M000205101

THE SPICY VEGAN COOKBOOK

THE
SPICY
VEGAN
COOKBOOK

More Than 200 Fiery Snacks, Dips, & Main Dishes for the Vegan Lifestyle

ADAMS MEDIA

Avon, Massachusetts

Copyright © 2014 by F+W Media, Inc.
All rights reserved.
This book, or parts thereof, may not be reproduced in any form without permission from the publisher; exceptions are made for brief excerpts used in published reviews.

Published by
Adams Media, a division of F+W Media, Inc.
57 Littlefield Street, Avon, MA 02322 U.S.A.
www.adamsmedia.com

Contains material adapted and abridged from *The Everything® Vegetarian Cookbook* by Jay Weinstein, copyright © 2002 by F+W Media, Inc., ISBN 10: 1-58062-640-8, ISBN 13: 978-1-58062-640-8; *The Everything® Vegetarian Slow Cooker Cookbook* by Amy Snyder and Justin Snyder, copyright © 2012 by F+W Media, Inc., ISBN 10: 1-4405-2858-6, ISBN 13: 978-1-4405-2858-3; *The Everything® Vegetarian Pressure Cooker Cookbook* by Amy Snyder and Justin Snyder, copyright © 2010 by F+W Media, Inc., ISBN 10: 1-4405-0672-8, ISBN 13: 978-1-4405-0672-7; *The Everything® Hot Sauce Book* by Angela Garbes, copyright © 2012 by F+W Media, Inc., ISBN 10: 1-4405-3011-4, ISBN 13: 978-1-4405-3011-1; *The Everything® Vegan Cookbook* by Jolinda Hackett with Lorena Novak Bull, copyright © 2010 by F+W Media, Inc., ISBN 10: 1-4405-0216-1, ISBN 13: 978-1-4405-0216-3; and *The Everything® Vegan Slow Cooker Cookbook* by Amy Snyder and Justin Snyder, copyright © 2012 by F+W Media, Inc., ISBN 10: 1-4405-4407-7, ISBN 13: 978-1-4405-4407-1.

ISBN 10: 1-4405-7323-9
ISBN 13: 978-1-4405-7323-1
epub eISBN 10: 1-4405-7324-7
epub eISBN 13: 978-1-4405-7324-8

Printed in the United States of America.

10 9 8 7 6 5 4 3 2 1

**Library of Congress
Cataloging-in-Publication Data**

The spicy vegan cookbook / Adams Media.
     pages cm
Includes index.
     ISBN 978-1-4405-7323-1 (pb) -- ISBN 1-4405-7323-9 (pb) -- ISBN 978-1-4405-7324-8 -- ISBN 1-4405-7324-7
     1. Vegan cooking. 2. Cooking (Spices) 3. Cooking (Hot pepper sauces) 4. International cooking. I. Adams Media, editors of compilation.
     TX837.S689 2014
     641.5'636--dc23

2013034695

Always follow safety and common-sense cooking protocol while using kitchen utensils, operating ovens and stoves, and handling uncooked food. If children are assisting in the preparation of any recipe, they should always be supervised by an adult.

Many of the designations used by manufacturers and sellers to distinguish their product are claimed as trademarks. Where those designations appear in this book and F+W Media was aware of a trademark claim, the designations have been printed with initial capital letters.

Cover image © 123RF.com.

*This book is available at quantity discounts for bulk purchases.
For information, please call
1-800-289-0963.*

CONTENTS

Chapter 5: Vegetables, Stir-Fries, and Sides 119

Chapter 6: Pasta, Rice, Grains, and Beans 151

PASTA

Chapter 7: Tofu, Seitan, TVP, and Tempeh 175

INTRODUCTION

Chipotle. Habanero. Jalapeño.

Today, hot and spicy ingredients like these are taking the culinary world by storm and are showing up on the menus of neighborhood diners and fine dining restaurants alike. But finding vegan dishes that satisfy your cravings for spice isn't always easy. Fortunately, *The Spicy Vegan Cookbook* offers more than 200 recipes guaranteed to give your palate the heat it's been looking for!

With vegan recipes ranging from Jalapeño Hash Browns to Garlic and Gingered Green Beans to Mango Chili Sorbet, you'll be able to fire up your table—no matter what meal you're eating! In addition, you'll find recipes like Coconut Curry Sauce, Cranberry Jalapeño Relish, Smoky Chipotle Salsa, and Homemade Chili Powder that show you how to make your own sauces, spices, salsas, and spreads so you can take anything on your menu and kick it up a notch.

Throughout the book, you'll find recipes with a variety of spices and levels of heat. Some recipes like Red Pepper Grits show restraint by calling for just a smattering of hot red pepper flakes, while others like the Five-Pepper Chili will have you calling the fire department to put out the heat the spicy habanero pepper left behind.

So whether you're looking for something just a little spicy or out-of-this-world hot, or if you're indulging in an early-morning breakfast or salivating over a late-night dessert, *The Spicy Vegan Cookbook* is sure to spice up your life!

CHAPTER 1

Breakfast and Brunch

Tofu Frittata

Frittatas are traditionally made with eggs, but you can use tofu instead for a cholesterol-free breakfast dish that is guaranteed to spice up your morning!

Serves 4

2 tablespoons olive oil
1 cup peeled and diced red
   potatoes
½ onion, diced
½ cup diced red pepper
½ cup diced green pepper
1 teaspoon minced jalapeño
1 clove garlic, minced
¼ cup parsley
1 (16-ounce) package firm tofu
½ cup unsweetened soymilk
4 teaspoons cornstarch
2 tablespoons nutritional yeast
1 teaspoon mustard
½ teaspoon turmeric
1 teaspoon salt
¼ teaspoon black pepper

1. Add the oil to a large pan and sauté the potatoes, onion, peppers, jalapeño, and garlic on medium heat for about 15–20 minutes.

2. Meanwhile, in a blender or food processor, combine the rest of the ingredients until smooth, then pour the mixture into the slow cooker with the potato mixture.

3. Cover, and cook on high heat for 4 hours, or until the frittata has firmed.

Chili Masala Tofu Scramble

Tofu scramble is an easy and versatile vegan breakfast. This version adds chili and curry to pump up the flavor. Toss in whatever veggies you have on hand—tomatoes, spinach, or diced broccoli would work well.

1. Cut or crumble pressed tofu into 1" cubes.

2. Sauté onion and garlic in olive oil for 1–2 minutes until onion is soft.

3. Add tofu, chili pepper, bell pepper, and mushrooms, stirring well to combine.

4. Add remaining ingredients, except nutritional yeast, and combine well. Allow to cook until tofu is lightly browned, about 6–8 minutes.

5. Remove from heat and stir in nutritional yeast if desired.

Serves 2

1 16-ounce block firm or extra-firm tofu, pressed
1 small onion, diced
2 cloves garlic, minced
2 tablespoons olive oil
1 small red chili pepper, minced
1 green bell pepper, chopped
¾ cup sliced mushrooms
1 tablespoon soy sauce
1 teaspoon curry powder
½ teaspoon cumin
¼ teaspoon turmeric
1 teaspoon nutritional yeast (optional)

🌶 THE NEXT DAY

Leftover tofu scramble makes an excellent lunch, or wrap leftovers (or planned-overs!) in a warmed flour tortilla to make breakfast-style burritos, perhaps with some salsa or beans. Why isn't it called "scrambled tofu" instead of "tofu scramble" if it's a substitute for scrambled eggs? This is one of the great conundrums of veganism.

Sunrise Tofu Scramble

Go gourmet with this spicy tofu scramble by substituting shiitake mushrooms and Japanese eggplant instead of the broccoli and button mushrooms.

Serves 4

1 (16-ounce) package firm tofu, drained and crumbled
½ cup chopped broccoli florets
½ cup sliced button mushrooms
2 tablespoons olive oil
2 teaspoons turmeric
1 teaspoon cumin
¼ teaspoon garlic powder
½ teaspoon red pepper flakes
2 cloves garlic, minced
1 teaspoon salt
¼ teaspoon black pepper
½ cup diced tomato
Juice of 1 lemon
2 tablespoons chopped fresh parsley

1. Add the tofu, broccoli, mushrooms, oil, turmeric, cumin, garlic powder, red pepper flakes, garlic, salt, and black pepper to a 4-quart slow cooker. Cover, and cook on low heat for 4 hours.

2. Add the tomato, lemon juice, and parsley to the scramble and serve.

Hot and Spicy Home Fries

Home fries are traditionally made in a pan or skillet on the stovetop, but they can be easily adapted for the slow cooker.

Place all ingredients in a 4-quart slow cooker, cover, and cook on high 2 hours.

Serves 6

2 pounds red potatoes, peeled and chopped
1 onion, chopped
1 green bell pepper, chopped
⅛ cup olive oil
½ teaspoon cumin
2 teaspoons paprika
1 teaspoon chili powder
1 teaspoon salt
¼ teaspoon black pepper

Jalapeño Hash Browns

The type of jalapeños you choose for this dish can make the heat vary greatly, so add what you like!

Serves 6

2 tablespoons olive oil
2 pounds red potatoes, peeled and shredded
1 onion, diced
¼ cup chopped pickled jalapeños
1 teaspoon salt
¼ teaspoon black pepper

Place all ingredients in a 4-quart slow cooker, cover, and cook on high 2 hours.

Onion, Pepper, and Poblano Hash

Use a cheese grater to achieve finely grated potatoes for this spicy dish.

Add all ingredients to a 4-quart slow cooker. Cover, and cook on high heat for 4 hours.

Serves 4

2 tablespoons olive oil
4 cups peeled and grated russet potatoes
½ onion, diced
1 poblano pepper, cored and diced
2 cloves garlic, minced
1 teaspoon chili powder
½ teaspoon paprika
½ teaspoon cumin
1 teaspoon salt
¼ teaspoon pepper

🔥 BETTER HASH BROWNS

After you have grated the potatoes for the hash browns, make sure to rinse them in a colander to get rid of the extra starch. Then, allow the potatoes to dry so they will get extra crispy in the slow cooker.

Potato Poblano Breakfast Burritos

With or without the optional ingredient, this hot and spicy breakfast is sure to fill you up!

Serves 2

2 tablespoons olive oil
2 small potatoes, diced small
2 poblano or Anaheim chilies, diced
1 teaspoon chili powder
Salt and pepper, to taste
1 tomato, diced
2 flour tortillas, warmed
Hot sauce, to taste
Grated vegan cheese (optional)

1. Heat olive oil in a pan and add potatoes and chilies, sautéing until potatoes are almost soft, about 6–7 minutes.

2. Add chili powder, salt, pepper, and tomato, and stir well to combine.

3. Continue cooking until potatoes and tomatoes are soft, another 4–5 minutes.

4. Wrap in warmed flour tortillas with hot sauce and a bit of vegan cheese if desired.

Spicy Breakfast Burrito

Tofu is a great alternative to eggs in breakfast dishes, and tofu is naturally cholesterol-free!

1. Add olive oil, tofu, onion, jalapeño, red bell pepper, and poblano pepper to a 4-quart slow cooker and sauté on high for 5–8 minutes.

2. Add the black beans, turmeric, cumin, chili powder, salt, and black pepper. Cover, and cook on low heat for 4 hours.

3. Scoop the filling onto the tortillas and add the avocado, tomatoes, cilantro, and salsa. Fold the sides of the tortillas in and roll up the burritos.

🔥 STEAMING TORTILLAS

For best results, steam tortillas on the stovetop using a steamer basket. If you're in a hurry, throw the tortillas into the microwave one at a time and heat for about 30 seconds.

Serves 4

2 tablespoons olive oil
1 (16-ounce) package firm tofu, drained and crumbled
¼ cup diced red onion
1 tablespoon minced jalapeño
¼ cup diced red bell pepper
¼ cup diced poblano pepper
1 cup cooked black beans, drained
2 teaspoons turmeric
1 teaspoon cumin
½ teaspoon chili powder
½ teaspoon salt
¼ teaspoon black pepper
4 flour tortillas
1 avocado, peeled and sliced
½ cup diced tomatoes
¼ cup chopped cilantro
½ cup chipotle salsa

Red Pepper Grits

Grits are a true southern staple, but this recipe has a slight twist and calls for Vegetable Broth and red pepper flakes.

Serves 6

2 cups stone-ground grits
3 cups water
3 cups Vegetable Broth (see
  Chapter 4)
2 tablespoons vegan margarine
2 teaspoons red pepper flakes
1 teaspoon salt
¼ teaspoon black pepper

Place all ingredients in a 4-quart slow cooker, cover, and cook on high 2 hours.

 CHOOSING GRITS

You may be most familiar with instant or fast-cooking grits, but those should be avoided in slow-cooker recipes. Choose stone-ground or whole-kernel grits instead; they will hold up better during the long cook time.

CHAPTER 2

Sauces, Spreads, Salsas, and Spices

SAUCES AND SPREADS

Carolina Barbecue Sauce

Coconut Curry Sauce

Easy Peanut Sauce

Easy Asian Dipping Sauce

Mole

Tempeh Mole

Tomatillo Sauce

Cranberry Jalapeño Relish

Spicy Vegetable Marinara

SALSAS

Simple Salsa

Rancheros Salsa

Pressure Cooker Tomatillo Salsa

Pico de Gallo

Roasted Tomatillo Salsa

Mango Habanero Salsa

Mango Citrus Salsa

Chile de Árbol Salsa

Pineapple Salsa

Raw Tomatillo Salsa

Smoky Chipotle Salsa

Peanut Salsa

Creamy Pumpkin Seed and Habanero Salsa

Mixed Chili Salsa

Roasted Corn Salsa

Guajillo Salsa

Avocado Salsa

Super Spicy Salsa

Zesty Black Bean Salsa

Black Bean Salsa

SPICES

Homemade Chili Powder

Berbere

Creole Seasoning Blend

Adobo Seasoning

Curry Powder

Ras El Hanout

Baharat

Carolina Barbecue Sauce

This spicy sauce has a more acidic taste than the sweeter, mainstream, ketchup-based sauces.

Serves 6

¼ cup vegan margarine
1 cup apple cider vinegar
⅓ cup brown sugar
1 tablespoon molasses
1 tablespoon mustard
2 teaspoons vegan Worcestershire sauce
⅛ teaspoon cayenne pepper

Add all of the ingredients to the slow cooker and cook on high heat for 1 hour, stirring occasionally.

Coconut Curry Sauce

Red curry paste is ideal for this recipe, but any variety will do.

1. In a 4-quart slow cooker, add all ingredients except cilantro. Cover, and cook on low heat for 2 hours.

2. Add the chopped cilantro and cook for an additional 30 minutes.

Serves 6

1 (14-ounce) can coconut milk
1 cup Vegetable Broth (see Chapter 4)
1 teaspoon soy sauce
1 tablespoon curry paste
1 tablespoon lime juice
2 cloves garlic, minced
½ teaspoon salt
¼ cup chopped cilantro

Easy Peanut Sauce

Choose a peanut butter that is free of added flavors and is as natural as possible, so that it won't distort the flavors in your dish.

Serves 6

1 cup smooth peanut butter
4 tablespoons maple syrup
½ cup sesame oil
1 teaspoon cayenne pepper
1½ teaspoons cumin
1 teaspoon garlic powder
1½ teaspoons salt
2 cups water

1. In a blender, add all ingredients except the water. Blend as you slowly add the water until you reach the desired consistency.

2. Pour the sauce into a 2-quart slow cooker and cook on low heat for 1 hour.

🔥 USES FOR PEANUT SAUCE

Peanut sauce can be used to dress Asian noodles such as udon or soba noodles. It may also be used as a dipping sauce for steamed broccoli or spring rolls.

Easy Asian Dipping Sauce

Tangy, salty, spicy, and a bit sour—this easy dipping sauce has it all! Use it for dipping vegan sushi! It also makes an excellent marinade for a baked tofu dish.

Whisk together all ingredients. Enjoy!

Yields ⅓ cup

¼ cup soy sauce

2 tablespoons rice vinegar

2 teaspoons sesame oil

1 teaspoon sugar

1 teaspoon minced fresh ginger

2 cloves garlic, minced and crushed

¼ teaspoon red pepper flakes, or to taste

Mole

Just like barbecue sauce in the United States, mole sauce recipes vary greatly by region, and no two are exactly the same.

Serves 6

2 tablespoons olive oil
½ onion, finely diced
3 cloves garlic, minced
1 teaspoon ground cumin
¼ teaspoon ground cinnamon
¼ teaspoon ground coriander
1 tablespoon chili powder
2 chipotles in adobo, seeded
    and minced
1 teaspoon salt
4 cups Vegetable Broth (see
    Chapter 4)
1 ounce vegan dark chocolate,
    chopped

1. In a sauté pan over medium heat, add the oil, onion, and garlic and sauté about 3 minutes. Add the cumin, cinnamon, and coriander and sauté for 1 minute.

2. Transfer the sautéed mixture to a 4-quart slow cooker. Add the chili powder, chipotles, and salt, then whisk in the Vegetable Broth. Finally, add the chocolate.

3. Cover, and cook on high heat for 2 hours.

Tempeh Mole

Mole is a type of Mexican sauce that is used on a variety of proteins. Try serving this Tempeh Mole with a bed of rice or warm flour tortillas.

1. Place the olive oil in a sauté pan over medium heat. Add the onion and garlic, then sauté for 2–3 minutes. When done, add the flour and whisk to create a roux.

2. Transfer the roux mixture and all remaining ingredients to a 4-quart slow cooker, cover, and cook on high for 2 hours.

Serves 4

2 tablespoons olive oil
1 onion, chopped
4 cloves garlic, minced
2 tablespoons flour
2 teaspoons Better Than Bouillon No Chicken Base
3 cups water
2 tablespoons chili powder
1 teaspoon cumin
1 teaspoon dried oregano
½ teaspoon cinnamon
⅓ cup vegan chocolate chips
½ teaspoon salt
⅛ teaspoon black pepper
1 (13-ounce) package tempeh, cut into bite-size squares

Tomatillo Sauce

Tomatillos look like small green tomatoes but are actually related to the gooseberry.

Serves 4

12 tomatillos, husked
Water, as needed
1 onion, diced
2 cloves garlic, minced
1 jalapeño, seeded and minced
½ tablespoon chopped fresh
 cilantro
1 teaspoon salt

1. Place the tomatillos in the slow cooker with enough water to cover them. Set the slow cooker to high and allow the tomatillos to cook for 1–2 hours or until tender. Drain the tomatillos.

2. Place the tomatillos, onion, garlic, jalapeño, cilantro, and salt in a food processor and purée. Place the mixture in a bowl and add water until it has the consistency of a sauce.

Cranberry Jalapeño Relish

If you can't take the heat, leave the jalapeños out of this recipe for a more traditional relish.

Add all ingredients to a 4-quart slow cooker, stir, cover, and cook on low heat for 2–3 hours.

Serves 6

1 (12-ounce) bag frozen cranberries
Juice of 2 oranges
Juice of 1 lemon
1 cup sugar
1 jalapeño, minced
⅛ cup water
¼ teaspoon salt
¼ black pepper

Spicy Vegetable Marinara

No Parmesan is needed to top off this hot and spicy vegetable marinara. Toss in a handful of TVP (textured vegetable protein) or browned, store-bought mock meat crumbles for a "meaty" sauce.

Serves 4

4 cloves garlic, minced
1 carrot, sliced thin
2 ribs celery, chopped
1 tablespoon + ½ teaspoon red pepper flakes, divided
2 tablespoons olive oil
1 (28-ounce) can diced or stewed tomatoes
1 (6-ounce) can tomato paste
1 teaspoon oregano
1 teaspoon parsley
2 tablespoons chopped fresh basil
2 bay leaves
2 jalapeños, diced
½ cup corn (optional)
½ cup sliced black olives
1 tablespoon balsamic vinegar
½ teaspoon salt

1. Heat garlic, carrot, celery, and 1 tablespoon red pepper flakes in olive oil over high heat, stirring frequently, for 4–5 minutes.

2. Reduce heat to low, then add tomatoes, tomato paste, oregano, parsley, basil, bay leaves, and jalapeños, stirring well to combine.

3. Cover, and heat for at least 30 minutes, stirring frequently.

4. Add corn if desired, olives, balsamic vinegar, ½ teaspoon red pepper flakes, and salt, and simmer for another 5 minutes uncovered.

5. Remove bay leaves before serving and adjust seasonings, to taste.

🔥 IN A PINCH

Don't have time to make marinara from scratch? Take 5 minutes to heat a store-bought variety on the stove and add in frozen veggies, Italian seasonings, and a bit of wine or balsamic vinegar for a fresh taste.

Simple Salsa

This simple, spicy condiment pairs magnificently with burritos, tacos, empanadas, tortilla chips, and all kinds of other Mexican savories.

Quarter the tomatoes. Cut out the inside viscera; reserve. Cut the remaining petals into a fine dice. Purée the insides in a food processor until smooth. Toss together with the tomato dice, the diced onion, jalapeños, lime juice, salt, pepper, and chipotle. Keeps in the refrigerator for 2 days, but is best served the day it's made.

Yields 1 cup

2 large tomatoes
1 small onion, finely diced
1 or 2 jalapeño peppers, finely chopped
½ teaspoon fresh-squeezed lime juice
Salt and freshly ground black pepper
½ teaspoon chipotle purée

Rancheros Salsa

This spicy salsa freezes exceptionally well. Consider making a double batch and storing half for later.

Yields 4 cups

2 tablespoons olive oil

1 medium white onion, roughly chopped

1 red bell pepper, roughly chopped

1 green bell pepper, roughly chopped

4 plum tomatoes, seeded and roughly chopped

1 tablespoon chopped garlic (about 4 cloves)

1 (14-ounce) can diced tomatoes in tomato purée

1 (7-ounce) can tomatillos, drained

1 (7-ounce) can green chilies, rinsed, drained, and roughly chopped

1 teaspoon chipotle purée

1 jalapeño pepper, seeded and finely chopped

¼ cup chopped cilantro

1 tablespoon frozen orange juice concentrate

1 teaspoon ground cumin, toasted in a dry pan until fragrant

1 teaspoon dried oregano

¼ teaspoon ground cinnamon

Salt and pepper, to taste

In a large, heavy-bottomed pot, heat the oil over medium-high heat until hot but not smoky. Add onion, peppers, and plum tomatoes; cook 5 minutes until onion is translucent. In a food processor, purée garlic, diced tomatoes, and tomatillos; add to onion mixture. Cook 5 minutes more. Add chilies, chipotle, jalapeño, and cilantro; stir in orange juice concentrate, cumin, oregano, cinnamon, salt, and pepper. Cook 5 minutes more. Remove from heat and enjoy.

Pressure Cooker Tomatillo Salsa

Serve this Pressure Cooker Tomatillo Salsa with corn tortilla chips or as an accompaniment to Black Bean Dip (see Chapter 3).

1. Cut the tomatillos in half and then place in the pressure cooker. Add enough water to cover the tomatillos.

2. Lock the lid into place; bring to high pressure and maintain for 2 minutes. Remove from heat and allow pressure to release naturally.

3. Add the drained, cooked tomatillos, jalapeños, onion, and cold water to a food processor or blender. Blend until well combined. Add the cilantro and salt and pulse until combined. Chill the salsa before serving.

Serves 8

1 pound tomatillos, paper removed
Water, as needed
2 jalapeños, stemmed, seeded, and chopped
½ onion, chopped
½ cup cold water
½ cup chopped cilantro
2 teaspoons salt

🔥 TOMATILLO

The tomatillo is the small yellowish or green fruit of a Mexican ground-cherry. Surprisingly, it is not a variety of tomato.

Pico de Gallo

This is a classic, fresh salsa that's easy to throw together just minutes before eating. This salsa tastes best in summer, when tomatoes are at their juiciest and most flavorful. For more spice, don't seed the chili peppers.

Yields 2½ cups

1 white onion, finely chopped

4 ripe tomatoes, seeded and finely chopped

3 jalapeño peppers, seeded and finely chopped

½ cup finely chopped cilantro leaves

1 tablespoon fresh lime juice

Salt, to taste

1. Combine all the ingredients in a bowl and mix thoroughly.

2. If there is time, let it sit in the refrigerator for 20 minutes.

♨ PICO DE GALLO: WHAT'S IN A NAME?

Pico de Gallo translates literally to "the beak of the rooster." The exact reason for the name is unknown, though perhaps it's because the red of the tomatoes is reminiscent of the bird's beak. Pico de Gallo is also beloved because it contains the three colors of the Mexican flag: red, white, and green.

Roasted Tomatillo Salsa

This is a relatively simple salsa, but taking the time to roast the tomatillos, chilies, garlic, and scallions gives the salsa an extra smoky and charred flavor that is well worth the extra time.

1. Remove the papery husks from the tomatillos and wash thoroughly.

2. Peel the garlic, but leave the cloves whole. Trim the root ends off the scallions.

3. On a comal or nonstick skillet, roast the tomatillos, chilies, garlic, and scallions until the tomatillos are softened and blackened.

4. Put all the vegetables into a blender with the cilantro, oregano, and salt. Blend until smooth.

5. Store in an airtight container in the refrigerator, where it will keep for up to 2 weeks.

Yields about 2½ cups

1 pound tomatillos
3 dried chiles de árbol
2 cloves garlic
3 scallions
Handful cilantro
Dried oregano, to taste
Salt, to taste

 WHAT IS A COMAL?

A comal is a smooth, flat griddle, usually cast iron, used throughout Mexico and Latin America to cook tortillas, toast spices, and roast chilies and vegetables. In many cultures, the comal is handed down from generation to generation, with the idea that the comal becomes better and more seasoned with age. If you don't have a comal, don't worry—a cast-iron pan will do.

Mango Habanero Salsa

This is a great salsa to enjoy in the summer. The juicy, sweet mangoes offer a nice contrast to the ultrahot habanero pepper.

Yields about 4 cups

3 tablespoons canola oil
3 cloves garlic, unpeeled
3 tomatillos, husked and washed
3 tomatoes, cored
1 red bell pepper
1 yellow bell pepper
1 orange habanero chili
1 medium red onion, finely chopped
¼ cup chopped cilantro leaves
¼ cup fresh lime juice
1 large mango, peeled, pitted, and cut into ¼" cubes
Kosher salt, to taste

1. Set oven to broil. Place a rack 6" from the heat source. Put the oil, garlic, tomatillos, tomatoes, bell peppers, chili, and onion in a large bowl and toss.

2. Transfer the ingredients to a foil-lined baking sheet. Broil them, turning a few times, until they are charred and blistered, about 10 minutes.

3. Transfer all but the peppers and chilies to a bowl; let cool. Continue broiling the peppers and chilies until soft, 3–5 minutes longer. Remove chilies from oven and let them steam in a covered bowl for a few minutes.

4. Peel the garlic. Stem, seed, and peel peppers and chili. Transfer all the roasted vegetables to a blender or food processor. Process until finely chopped.

5. Transfer the salsa to a bowl and stir in red onion, cilantro, lime juice, and mango. Season with salt.

Mango Citrus Salsa

Salsa has a variety of uses, and this recipe adds color and variety to your usual chips and dip or Mexican dishes.

1. Gently toss together all ingredients.

2. Allow to sit for at least 15 minutes before serving to allow flavors to mingle.

Yields 2 cups

1 mango, chopped
2 tangerines, chopped
½ red bell pepper, chopped
½ red onion, minced
3 cloves garlic, minced
½ jalapeño pepper, minced
2 tablespoons lime juice
½ teaspoon salt
¼ teaspoon black pepper
3 tablespoons chopped fresh
 cilantro

Chile de Árbol Salsa

Chiles de árbol are a staple in many salsas because of their strong heat and naturally subtle, smoky flavor. This salsa puts those flavors at the forefront.

Yields 2 cups

½ pound Roma tomatoes
½ pound tomatillos, husked and washed
1 cup (about 30–40) chiles de árbol
½ bunch cilantro, leaves only, roughly chopped
1 medium white onion, chopped
4 cloves garlic, peeled and lightly smashed
2 cups water
1 teaspoon salt

1. Set oven to broil. Place tomatoes and tomatillos on a baking sheet. Broil, turning occasionally, until they are charred, 10–12 minutes. Transfer to a saucepan.

2. Add the remaining ingredients to the saucepan. Bring mixture to a boil and cook until the onion is soft, about 12 minutes.

3. Transfer the sauce to a blender or food processor. Purée until smooth.

4. Strain the salsa into a bowl and serve.

5. Store leftover salsa in the refrigerator, where it will keep for about a week.

Pineapple Salsa

Another great tropical salsa that's especially nice in the summer. If you can, let it sit for 30 minutes before serving to give all the flavors time to mix.

1. Toss all the ingredients together in a large bowl and mix well.

2. Serve immediately or cover and chill until ready to use.

Yields 2 cups

2 cups diced fresh pineapple
½ cup chopped cilantro
¼ cup finely chopped red onion
1 serrano pepper, seeded and finely chopped
Juice and zest of 1 lime
¼ teaspoon kosher salt

Raw Tomatillo Salsa

This simple salsa, called *cruda*, is probably the easiest way to make a salsa from tomatillos. This sauce may seem a bit thin at first, but it will thicken as it stands.

Yields 1½ cups

1 pound (around 20) tomatillos, husked and washed
4 serrano chilies, seeded and roughly chopped
1 cup roughly chopped cilantro leaves and stems
1 large clove garlic, peeled and roughly chopped
Salt, to taste

1. Put the tomatillos in a small pan, just barely cover them with water, and bring to a simmer. Simmer for about 10 minutes or until they are softened. Drain, but reserve ½ cup of the cooking water.

2. Combine ½ cup of the cooking water, chilies, cilantro, and garlic in a blender. Blend until almost smooth.

3. Add the cooked tomatillos in small batches, blending briefly after each one. The sauce should be chunky and rough.

4. Transfer to a bowl and add salt.

Smoky Chipotle Salsa

Chipotles add a surprise smoky flavor to this salsa, which also has plenty of sweetness from roasted tomatoes. Serve this as a table salsa with chips for a nice change of pace.

1. Roast tomatoes, onion, chilies, and garlic on a comal or cast-iron skillet until they are nearly blackened.

2. Place the vegetables and chilies in a blender and add a little water. Blend until smooth. Season with salt, to taste.

Yields about 2 cups

8 medium tomatoes
1 yellow onion, halved
4 dried chipotle chilies
2 cloves garlic
½–1 cup water
Salt, to taste

Peanut Salsa

This unusual salsa originated on the Gulf Coast of Mexico. Spread this hot sauce on top of warm tortillas or rice.

Yields 2 cups

1 cup roasted unsalted peanuts, shelled
2 cups water, divided
4 canned chipotle chilies in adobo, roughly chopped
2 cloves garlic, peeled and roughly chopped
2 black peppercorns
2 cloves
2 tablespoons vegetable oil
Salt, to taste

1. Grind the peanuts in a coffee grinder or food processor until they are a fine powder.

2. Put ½ cup of water into a blender, along with the chilies, garlic, and spices. Blend well.

3. Heat the vegetable oil, then fry the blended ingredients in it for 4 minutes, stirring constantly so they do not stick to the bottom. Gradually stir in the ground peanuts and cook for another 2 minutes.

4. Add the rest of the water and salt and continue cooking, stirring and scraping the bottom of the pan, for another 5 minutes. Remove from heat and serve.

Creamy Pumpkin Seed and Habanero Salsa

This salsa, called *sikil pak*, is a traditional Mayan recipe from the Yucatan Peninsula. It's incredibly creamy, yet there is no trace of dairy. Be careful when handling the roasted habanero here—consider gloves!

1. Toast the pepitas in a dry, hot skillet or in the oven until golden brown.

2. Char the tomatoes, onion, and habanero on a comal or cast-iron skillet until they are softened and a little black, about 5 minutes. Carefully seed and roughly chop the habanero.

3. Put all the ingredients into a food processor or blender. Pulse until well blended. The salsa should be thick and creamy. Add a little water to thin if necessary.

Yields 1½ cups

1 cup pumpkin seeds (pepitas), toasted
3 tomatoes
½ large white onion, thickly sliced
1 habanero chili
½ cup cilantro leaves
Salt, to taste
Water, as needed

Mixed Chili Salsa

This raw salsa is bright and colorful. If you are lucky enough to live near a market that sells a variety of chilies, be sure to make this. Feel free to vary it with whatever chilies are fresh and available.

Yields 1½ cups

1 poblano chili, seeded and finely chopped

1 red jalapeño, seeded and finely chopped

2 yellow chilies (such as a güero or Anaheim), seeded and finely chopped

2 serrano chilies, seeds intact, finely chopped

½ white onion, finely chopped

2 tomatoes, seeded and finely chopped

3 tablespoons fresh lime juice

½ teaspoon dried oregano

Salt, to taste

1. Mix all the ingredients together in a nonreactive bowl.

2. Set aside for 1 hour before serving.

🌶 GÜERO

Güero chilies are medium-hot peppers that are a yellow color. They are also sometimes called goldspike chilies. Güero translates from Spanish to "blonde," though it is also called out on the streets in Mexico as a generic nickname (not necessarily derogatively) for light-haired or light-skinned tourists and locals.

Roasted Corn Salsa

This is a great spicy salsa to make in summer, when corn on the cob is bursting with sweetness. You can serve with chips or put it on tacos, but it's also hearty enough to be a side dish.

1. Shuck the corn cobs and shave the corn kernels from the cob. Heat a dry, large, cast-iron skillet over medium-high heat and pan-roast corn, stirring occasionally until golden brown, about 8–9 minutes. Transfer to a bowl.

2. Cook the white part of scallions in margarine with garlic, 1 teaspoon of salt, ½ teaspoon each of cumin and chili powder, and a few pinches of black pepper. Cook until scallions are tender, about 3 minutes.

3. Remove pan from heat and stir in corn, tomatoes, jalapeños, green parts of scallions, and remaining spices.

4. Transfer to bowl. Serve warm or chill in the refrigerator before serving.

Yields 3½ cups

3 ears fresh corn
4 scallions, white and green parts separated and thinly sliced
2 tablespoons unsalted vegan margarine
2 cloves garlic, peeled and minced
1½ teaspoons kosher salt, divided
1½ teaspoons ground cumin, divided
1 teaspoon chili powder, divided
Pepper, to taste
2 plum tomatoes, seeded and finely diced
2 fresh jalapeños, with seeds, finely diced

Guajillo Salsa

This is a salsa of medium heat, with plenty of nice chili flavor from the guajillos. You can serve it as a table salsa or heat it with two tablespoons of chili oil to make a hot sauce.

Yields 3 cups

½ pound dried guajillo chilies
3 cups hot water
5 large cloves garlic, roasted
1 teaspoon ground cumin
1 teaspoon kosher salt
½ pound Roma tomatoes
2 teaspoons toasted pumpkin
    seeds
⅓ cup apple cider vinegar
1 teaspoon dried oregano

1. Remove the stems from the guajillos and lightly toast them on a comal or cast-iron skillet. Transfer them to a bowl and cover with hot water. Let them sit for at least 15 minutes.

2. When the chilies are softened, remove them from the water and chop roughly. Save a bit of the chili soaking water.

3. Purée the chilies with the remaining ingredients until the mixture forms a paste. Add a little chili water to thin if necessary.

🔥 PUMPKIN SEEDS

Called pepitas *in Spanish, pumpkin seeds are commonly used in Mexican cuisine as a thickener for sauces. Along with adding body to salsas and moles, pumpkin seeds add a warm, nutty flavor to dishes.*

Avocado Salsa

This is a tangy green salsa made smooth and silky by the addition of avocados. You can use it on tacos or in enchiladas, but you just might find yourself eating it straight with a spoon. Be sure to use soft, ripe avocados.

1. Combine the tomatillos, jalapeños, and garlic in a saucepan, along with a bit of water. Bring to a boil, then reduce heat and simmer for 10 minutes. Remove from heat and let cool a bit.

2. Place the mixture, along with avocados, cilantro, and salt in a food processor or blender. Blend until smooth. Add a little water if necessary to loosen mixture from blender blades.

3. Pour into a bowl and stir in the vegan sour cream.

Yields 4 cups

6 tomatillos, husked and washed, coarsely chopped
2 jalapeños, coarsely chopped
3 cloves garlic
Water, as needed
3 medium-size ripe avocados, peeled, pitted, and thinly sliced
5 sprigs cilantro
1 teaspoon salt
1½ cups vegan sour cream

Super Spicy Salsa

You can use this hot and spicy salsa in so many ways. It's wonderful in frittatas and delicious as a garnish for chili.

Yields ¼ cup

2 jalapeño peppers, minced
1 habanero pepper, minced
1 green bell pepper, minced
4 cloves garlic, minced
1 red onion, chopped
5 ripe tomatoes, chopped
3 tablespoons lemon juice
¼ teaspoon salt
⅛ teaspoon white pepper
¼ cup chopped fresh cilantro

1. In large bowl, combine jalapeños, habanero pepper, bell pepper, garlic, red onion, and tomatoes.

2. In small bowl, combine lemon juice, salt, and pepper; stir to dissolve salt. Add to tomato mixture along with cilantro.

3. Cover, and refrigerate for 3–4 hours before serving.

Zesty Black Bean Salsa

This hearty, filling, spicy salsa gets its body from fiber-rich black beans.

1. Place onion, cilantro, parsley, and jalapeño in food processor; finely chop.

2. In medium bowl, combine onion mixture, black beans, and tomatoes.

3. In separate small bowl, whisk together lime juice, olive oil, and black pepper. Pour over beans; mix well. Chill before serving.

Serves 10

1 cup chopped red onion
¼ cup cilantro
¼ cup parsley
1 jalapeño pepper
1½ cups black beans, cooked
4 cups chopped tomatoes
3 tablespoons lime juice
2 tablespoons olive oil
Freshly ground black pepper

🔥 USING CANNED BEANS VERSUS COOKING YOUR OWN

Canned beans are very convenient and can save you time. Keep in mind sodium content of recipes will be higher with canned beans. Reduce sodium content in canned beans by draining and thoroughly rinsing with cold water before using.

Black Bean Salsa

This slow-cooker recipe makes a lot of salsa, so it's great for parties or large gatherings.

Serves 8

1 (16-ounce) bag dried black beans
Enough water to cover beans by 1"
4 teaspoons salt, divided
2 (15-ounce) cans tomatoes, drained
1 cup corn
1 onion, diced
1 jalapeño, minced
3 cloves garlic, minced
3 teaspoons apple cider vinegar
2 teaspoons sugar
¼ teaspoon black pepper
¼ cup chopped cilantro

1. Rinse the black beans, then soak overnight. Drain the water and rinse the beans again.

2. In a large pot, add the beans and cover with water. Boil on high heat for 10 minutes, then drain.

3. Add the black beans, water, and 2 teaspoons salt to a 4-quart slow cooker. Cover, and cook on low heat for about 5–6 hours. Check the beans at about 5 hours and continue cooking if necessary.

4. Once the beans are done, drain in a colander and allow to cool to room temperature.

5. In a large bowl, combine the beans with the rest of the ingredients.

Homemade Chili Powder

Of course you can go to any store and buy chili powder in a bottle, but where's the fun in that? Making your own is easy and, best of all, you can customize it however you like. Here's a basic recipe, but feel free to tinker with it and add more heat or use different types of chilies.

1. Lightly toast the chilies on a comal or cast-iron skillet until they puff slightly.

2. Put chilies in a food processor or blender and blend until they form a fine powder. Transfer to a bowl.

3. Add the remaining ingredients and stir well until thoroughly mixed.

4. Store in an airtight container for up to 6 months.

Yields 1 cup

4 dried ancho chilies, stemmed, seeded, and roughly chopped
4–5 dried chiles de árbol, stemmed and seeded
2 tablespoons ground cumin
2 tablespoons garlic powder
1 tablespoon dried oregano
1 teaspoon paprika (hot or sweet)
½ teaspoon cayenne pepper

🔥 ORIGINS OF CHILI POWDER

No one knows the exact origins of chili powder, but the original version of what you see in supermarkets was created in the United States sometime in the nineteenth century. Chili powder was developed as the way to flavor southwestern staple chili con carne. For every household that made chili, there was likely a unique chili powder blend.

Berbere

This complex, heady spice mix is the foundation for all Ethiopian cooking. There are a lot of ingredients, but it's well worth all the grinding and mixing. Try to use whole spices as much as possible, and feel free to adjust seasoning to your liking.

Yields 1 cup

1 teaspoon fenugreek seeds
½ cup dried red chilies such as
   japones or chiles de árbol
½ cup hot paprika
2 tablespoons salt
1 teaspoon ground ginger
2 teaspoons onion powder
1 teaspoon ground green
   cardamom
1 teaspoon ground nutmeg
1 teaspoon garlic powder
¼ teaspoon ground cloves
½ teaspoon ground cinnamon
¼ teaspoon ground allspice

1. Grind the seeds and chilies in a spice or coffee grinder. Be careful not to inhale all the bits of spice that will be released during the process.

2. Pour all the spices into a bowl and stir well until completely combined.

3. Store in an airtight container in the refrigerator for up to 3 months.

🔥 BERBERE

In Ethiopia, the process of making berbere can take days—even up to 1 week. Chilies are often dried in the sun for multiple days, then ground by hand with a mortar and pestle. Then the chilies are combined with other spices and left to dry in the sun again. While the fundamental flavors are the same, families each have their own unique berbere recipe and mix.

Creole Seasoning Blend

The building block for so many great southern dishes like gumbo and jambalaya, this spice blend also works great as a rub for barbecued veggies.

1. Combine all ingredients in a bowl and stir well.

2. Store in an airtight container for up to 6 months.

Yields about 1 cup

5 tablespoons hot paprika

3 tablespoons kosher salt

2 tablespoons garlic powder

2 tablespoons onion powder

2 tablespoons dried oregano

2 tablespoons dried basil

2 tablespoons black pepper

1 tablespoon dried thyme

1 tablespoon cayenne pepper

1 tablespoon white pepper

Adobo Seasoning

Adobo is a spice mixture that is used throughout Latin America and the Caribbean. Try it on veggies—then grill, roast, or fry.

Yields 1½ cups

6 tablespoons kosher salt

6 tablespoons granulated garlic

2 tablespoons ground black pepper

2 tablespoons onion powder

2 tablespoons ground cumin

2 tablespoons ground coriander

2 tablespoons chili powder (a smoky chipotle powder would be good, but use whatever you have on hand)

¼ teaspoon allspice

½ teaspoon dried oregano

1. Put all ingredients in a bowl and stir until thoroughly combined.

2. Store in an airtight container for up to a year.

Curry Powder

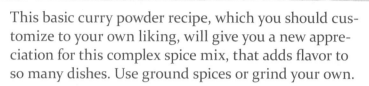

This basic curry powder recipe, which you should customize to your own liking, will give you a new appreciation for this complex spice mix, that adds flavor to so many dishes. Use ground spices or grind your own.

1. Grind whatever spices need grinding.

2. Combine all ingredients and stir until well combined.

3. Store in an airtight container for up to 6 months.

Yields 1 cup

6 tablespoons ground coriander
4 tablespoons ground cumin
2 tablespoons black pepper
2 tablespoons ground cinnamon
1 tablespoon turmeric
1 tablespoon ground ginger
1 tablespoon cayenne pepper
1 teaspoon ground nutmeg
1 teaspoon ground cloves

 TURMERIC

Turmeric is the spice that gives all curry powder its distinct yellow-orange hue. Turmeric has an astringent yet earthy flavor, akin to mustard or horseradish but more mellow. Its strong color will dye any food that it is sprinkled on. You might also find fresh turmeric at specialty grocery stores, where it looks similar to its cousin, ginger.

Ras El Hanout

The Arabic phrase *ras el hanout* means "top of the shop" and refers to a spice owner's special blend of his best spices. It's an essential Moroccan spice mix and some versions have upward of 20 or even 30 ingredients.

Yields ¼ cup

1 teaspoon ground cloves
1 teaspoon ground ginger
1 teaspoon ground cardamom
1 teaspoon ground mace
1 teaspoon ground nutmeg
1 teaspoon ground black pepper
1 teaspoon ground cinnamon
1 teaspoon ground allspice
1 teaspoon ground turmeric
1 teaspoon hot paprika

1. Combine all the spices and stir until thoroughly mixed.

2. Store in an airtight container for up to 6 months.

Baharat

Baharat is a spice mix used throughout the Middle East: Lebanon, Syria, Israel, Jordan. Its name simply means "spice" in Arabic. There are endless variations, so feel free to experiment. Try Baharat on different vegetables.

1. Combine all spices and mix well.

2. Store in an airtight container for up to 6 months.

Yields ½ cup

2 tablespoons freshly ground pepper

2 tablespoons hot paprika

1 tablespoon ground coriander seeds

1 tablespoon ground cumin

1 tablespoon ground cloves

1 tablespoon ground mint

2 teaspoons ground nutmeg

1 teaspoon ground cinnamon

CHAPTER 3

Salads, Hors d'Oeuvres, and Snacks

SALADS

Spicy Southwestern Two-Bean Salad

Thai Orange Peanut Dressing

Cucumber Cilantro Salad

Messy Taco Salad

Spicy Sweet Cucumber Salad

Lemon Cumin Potato Salad

Black Bean and Barley Taco Salad

Spiced Couscous Salad with Bell Pepper and Zucchini

HORS D'OEUVRES AND SNACKS

Eggplant Baba Ghanoush

Spicy Seitan Buffalo Strips

Garlic Confit

Roasted Red Pepper Hummus

Pintos, Cerveza, and Lime Dip

Nacho "Cheese" Dip

Frijole Dip

Black Bean Dip

Tofu and Portobello Enchiladas

Portobello and Pepper Fajitas

Chickpea Soft Tacos

Southwest Sweet Potato Enchiladas

Caramelized Onion and Mushroom Cheeseless Quesadillas

Spicy Southwestern Two-Bean Salad

This cold bean salad with Tex-Mex flavors is even better the next day—if it lasts that long!

Serves 6

1 (15-ounce) can black beans, drained and rinsed

1 (15-ounce) can kidney beans, drained and rinsed

1 red or yellow bell pepper, chopped

1 large tomato, diced

⅔ cup corn (fresh, canned, or frozen)

1 red onion, diced

⅓ cup olive oil

¼ cup lime juice

½ teaspoon chili powder

½ teaspoon garlic powder

¼ teaspoon cayenne pepper

½ teaspoon salt

¼ cup chopped fresh cilantro

1 avocado, diced

1. In a large bowl, combine the black beans, kidney beans, bell pepper, tomato, corn, and onion.

2. In a separate small bowl, whisk together the olive oil, lime juice, chili powder, garlic powder, cayenne, and salt.

3. Pour dressing over bean mixture, tossing to coat. Stir in fresh cilantro.

4. Chill for at least 1 hour before serving to allow flavors to mingle.

5. Add avocado and gently toss again just before serving.

 MAKE IT A PASTA SALAD

Omit the avocado and add some cooked pasta and extra dressing to turn it into a high-protein Tex-Mex pasta salad!

Thai Orange Peanut Dressing

This recipe is a sweet-and-spicy take on traditional Thai and Indonesian peanut and satay sauce. Add a bit less liquid to use this salad dressing as a dip for veggies.

Whisk together all ingredients until smooth and creamy, adding more or less liquid to achieve desired consistency.

Yields ¾ cup

¼ cup peanut butter at room temperature
¼ cup orange juice
2 tablespoons soy sauce
2 tablespoons rice vinegar
2 tablespoons water
½ teaspoon garlic powder
½ teaspoon sugar
1 teaspoon red pepper flakes

Cucumber Cilantro Salad

In this recipe, cooling cucumbers and cold, creamy yogurt are coupled with a dash of cayenne pepper for a salad that keeps you guessing.

Serves 3

4 cucumbers, diced
2 tomatoes, chopped
½ red onion, diced small
1 cup soy yogurt, plain or lemon
  flavored
1 tablespoon lemon juice
2 tablespoons chopped fresh
  cilantro
Salt and pepper, to taste
¼ teaspoon cayenne pepper

1. Toss together all ingredients, stirring well to combine.

2. Chill for at least 2 hours before serving to allow flavors to marinate. Toss again just before serving.

Messy Taco Salad

If you're bored by the usual salads but still want something light and green, try this taco salad. The taste and texture is best with iceberg lettuce, but if you want something more nutritious, use a blend of half iceberg and half romaine. Top with a handful of shredded vegan cheese if you'd like.

1. Combine the lettuce, olives, corn, and jalapeño pepper or green chilies in a large bowl.

2. Warm the beans slightly on the stove or in the microwave, just until softened. Combine beans with taco sauce or hot sauce, salsa, and mayonnaise, breaking up the beans and mixing to form a thick sauce.

3. Combine bean mixture with lettuce, stirring to combine as much as possible. Add tortilla chips and avocado if desired, and stir gently to combine. Add 1–2 dashes of extra hot sauce, to taste.

Serves 4

2 heads iceberg lettuce, chopped
½ cup sliced black olives
½ cup corn
1 jalapeño pepper, seeded and sliced, or 2 tablespoons canned green chilies
1 can refried black beans
2 tablespoons taco sauce or 1 teaspoon hot sauce
¼ cup salsa
¼ cup vegan mayonnaise
10–12 tortilla chips, crumbled
1 avocado, diced (optional)

🔥 BAKED TORTILLA CHIPS

Why not make your own tortilla chips! Slice whole-wheat tortillas into strips or triangles, and arrange in a single layer on a baking sheet. Drizzle with olive oil for a crispier chip, and season with a bit of salt and garlic powder if you want, or just bake them plain. It'll take about 5–6 minutes on each side in a 300°F oven.

Spicy Sweet Cucumber Salad

This Japanese cucumber salad is cool and refreshing, but with a bit of spice. Enjoy it as a healthy afternoon snack, or as a fresh accompaniment to takeout.

Serves 2

2 cucumbers, thinly sliced
¾ teaspoon salt
¼ cup rice wine vinegar
1 teaspoon sugar or 1 tablespoon agave nectar
1 teaspoon sesame oil
¼ teaspoon red pepper flakes
½ onion, thinly sliced

1. In a large, shallow container or baking sheet, spread the cucumbers in single layer and sprinkle with salt. Allow to sit at least 10 minutes.

2. Drain any excess water from the cucumbers.

3. Whisk together the rice wine vinegar, sugar or agave nectar, oil, and red pepper flakes.

4. Pour dressing over the cucumbers, add onions, and toss gently.

5. Allow to sit at least 10 minutes before serving to allow flavors to mingle.

Lemon Cumin Potato Salad

A mayonnaise-free potato salad with exotic flavors, this spicy dish is delicious either hot or cold.

1. Heat onion in olive oil just until soft. Add cumin and potatoes, and cook for just 1 minute, stirring well to combine. Remove from heat.

2. Whisk together the lemon juice and Dijon mustard and pour over potatoes, tossing gently to coat. Add scallion, cayenne pepper, and cilantro if desired, and combine well.

3. Chill before serving.

Serves 4

1 small yellow onion, diced
2 tablespoons olive oil
1½ teaspoons cumin
4 large cooked potatoes, chopped
3 tablespoons lemon juice
2 teaspoons Dijon mustard
1 scallion, chopped
¼ teaspoon cayenne pepper
2 tablespoons chopped fresh cilantro (optional)

🔥 THE FAMILY RECIPE

Traditional American potato salads are easy to veganize, so if you have a family favorite, take a look at the ingredients. Substitute vegan mayonnaise or sour cream for regular, omit the eggs, and use mock meats in place of the bacon bits or other meats.

Black Bean and Barley Taco Salad

Adding barley to a taco salad gives a bit of a whole-grain and fiber boost to this low-fat, spicy recipe.

Serves 2

1 (15-ounce) can black beans, drained

½ teaspoon cumin

½ teaspoon oregano

2 tablespoons lime juice

1 teaspoon hot sauce

1 cup cooked barley

1 head iceberg lettuce, shredded

¾ cup salsa

Handful tortilla chips, crumbled

2 tablespoons vegan Italian dressing (optional)

1. Mash together the beans, cumin, oregano, lime juice, and hot sauce until beans are mostly mashed, then combine with barley.

2. Layer lettuce with beans and barley and top with salsa and tortilla chips. Drizzle with Italian dressing if desired.

Spiced Couscous Salad with Bell Pepper and Zucchini

This salad can act as a full meal for lunch or dinner, or a side salad, depending on how hungry you are!

1. Combine Vegetable Broth and couscous and bring to a boil. Add cumin, turmeric, paprika, and cayenne pepper, and stir to combine.

2. Turn off heat, cover, and allow to sit for at least 15 minutes until couscous is soft and liquid is absorbed. Fluff couscous with a fork and add lemon juice.

3. Sauté zucchinis, bell peppers, and garlic in olive oil just until soft; combine with couscous.

4. Add parsley, taste, and season lightly with salt and pepper.

Serves 4

2 cups Vegetable Broth (see Chapter 4)
2 cups couscous
1 teaspoon cumin
½ teaspoon turmeric
½ teaspoon paprika
¼ teaspoon cayenne pepper
1 tablespoon lemon juice
2 zucchinis, sliced
1 red bell pepper, chopped
1 yellow bell pepper, chopped
3 cloves garlic, minced
2 tablespoons olive oil
2 tablespoons chopped fresh parsley
Salt and pepper, to taste

Eggplant Baba Ghanoush

Whip up a batch of this Eggplant Baba Ghanoush and some Roasted Red Pepper Hummus (see recipe in this chapter) and make a spicy Mediterranean appetizer spread. Don't forget some vegan pita bread to dip into your dish.

Yields 1½ cups

2 medium eggplants
3 tablespoons olive oil, divided
2 tablespoons lemon juice
¼ cup tahini
3 cloves garlic
½ teaspoon cumin
½ teaspoon chili powder
¼ teaspoon salt
1 tablespoon chopped fresh
  parsley

1. Preheat oven to 400°F. Slice eggplants in half lengthwise and prick several times with a fork.

2. Place on a baking sheet and drizzle with 1 tablespoon olive oil. Bake for 30 minutes, or until soft. Allow to cool slightly.

3. Remove inner flesh and place in a bowl.

4. Using a large fork or potato masher, mash eggplant together with remaining ingredients until almost smooth.

5. Adjust seasonings, to taste.

Spicy Seitan Buffalo Strips

Most bottled buffalo wing sauces contain butter, so be sure to read the label or make your own by following the steps below.

1. Place the vegan margarine in a small bowl and microwave for 30 seconds, or until melted.

2. Add the hot sauce, vinegar, and garlic powder and stir well.

3. In a 4-quart slow cooker, add the prepared hot sauce mixture and Chick'n Strips and cook on low heat for 1 hour.

Serves 6

⅓ cup vegan margarine
⅓ cup hot sauce
1 tablespoon vinegar
1 teaspoon garlic powder
2 (7-ounce) packages Gardein Chick'n Strips

🔥 SERVING STRIPS

Faux buffalo chicken strips can be added to sandwiches or salads, but if you'd like to serve them as an appetizer or snack, place in a small basket lined with parchment paper and add sides of celery sticks, carrot sticks, and vegan ranch dressing.

Garlic Confit

Use this garlic in place of fresh garlic in recipes where you want a little spice, or enjoy it smashed and spread on toasted bread.

Yields 5 heads garlic

2–3 cups olive oil
5 heads garlic, cloves peeled
3 dried red chilies

1. Add all ingredients to a 4-quart slow cooker. Make sure there is enough oil to cover all the garlic cloves. Place the cover on the slow cooker and cook on low heat for 4 hours, or until the garlic is tender.

2. Remove the garlic with a slotted spoon and place in canning jars. Pour the oil over the garlic and seal the top.

🔥 PRESERVING GARLIC

Garlic confit is a great and easy way to preserve garlic when it is in season and at its peak. Garlic prepared using this method can be jarred and stored for up to 3 months.

Roasted Red Pepper Hummus

You'll rarely meet a vegan who doesn't love hummus in one form or another. As a veggie dip or sandwich spread, this spicy hummus is always a favorite. Up the cayenne pepper in this recipe if that's your thing, and don't be ashamed to lick the spoon.

Process all ingredients together in a blender or food processor until smooth, scraping the sides down as needed.

Yields 1½ cups

1 (15-ounce) can chickpeas, drained
⅓ cup tahini
⅔ cup chopped roasted red peppers
3 tablespoons lemon juice
2 tablespoons olive oil
2 cloves garlic
½ teaspoon cumin
⅓ teaspoon salt
¼ teaspoon cayenne pepper

♨ DO-IT-YOURSELF ROASTED RED PEPPERS

Sure, you can buy them in a jar, but it's easy to roast your own. Here's how: Fire up your oven to 450°F (or use the broiler setting) and drizzle a few whole peppers with olive oil. Bake for 30 minutes, turning over once. Direct heat will also work if you have a gas stove. Hold the peppers with tongs over the flame until lightly charred. Let your peppers cool, then remove the skin before making hummus.

Pintos, Cerveza, and Lime Dip

If you don't have a Mexican beer on hand when making this spicy dip, a domestic beer will work just fine.

Serves 6

2 tablespoons olive oil
½ onion, diced
3 cloves garlic, minced
½ pound dry pinto beans
3 cups water + additional water
  for processing
1 (12-ounce) Mexican beer
1 fresh jalapeño, minced
Juice of 2 limes
¼ teaspoon salt
⅛ teaspoon black pepper

1. Add the olive oil to the slow cooker and sauté the onion and garlic on high heat for 3–4 minutes.

2. Add the dry pinto beans, 3 cups of water, and beer to the slow cooker, cover, and cook on high heat for 4–5 hours, or until the beans are tender. Drain the pinto beans.

3. In a food processor, purée the pinto beans, minced jalapeño, lime juice, salt, and pepper, adding enough water to create a smooth consistency. Serve hot or at room temperature.

Nacho "Cheese" Dip

Peanut butter in cheese sauce? Absolutely! Just a touch of peanut butter gives a creamy and nutty layer of flavor in this spicy sauce, and helps it to thicken nicely. Use this sauce to dress plain steamed veggies or make homemade nachos.

Yields about 1 cup

3 tablespoons vegan margarine
1 cup unsweetened soymilk
¾ teaspoon garlic powder
½ teaspoon onion powder
½ teaspoon salt
1 tablespoon peanut butter
¼ cup flour
¼ cup nutritional yeast
¾ cup salsa
2 tablespoons chopped canned jalapeño peppers

1. Heat margarine and soymilk together in a pan over low heat. Add garlic powder, onion powder, and salt, stirring to combine. Add peanut butter and stir until melted.

2. Whisk in flour, 1 tablespoon at a time, until smooth. Heat until thickened, about 5–6 minutes.

3. Stir in nutritional yeast, salsa, and jalapeño peppers.

4. Allow to cool slightly before serving, as cheese sauce will thicken as it cools.

🔥 CHILI CHEESE

Add a can of store-bought vegan chili for a chili cheese dip, or smother some french fries to make chili cheese fries.

Frijole Dip

For best results, serve this spicy slow-cooker dip immediately after cooking or reheat if it cools. Keep in mind that if you make it the night before serving, you allow the spices time to mingle, which results in a spicier dish!

Serves 12

2 (15-ounce) cans pinto beans, drained
1½ cups water
1 tablespoon olive oil
1 small onion, peeled and diced
3 cloves garlic, peeled and minced
1 cup diced tomatoes
1 teaspoon chipotle powder
½ teaspoon cumin
¼ cup finely chopped fresh cilantro
Salt, to taste
1 cup vegan Monterey jack cheese

1. In a 4-quart slow cooker, add the beans, water, olive oil, onion, and garlic. Cover, and cook on low heat for 1 hour.

2. Mash the beans until about ½ are smooth and ½ are still chunky.

3. Add all remaining ingredients, stir well, and cook for an additional 30 minutes.

Black Bean Dip

To give this pressure cooker dip an extra kick, you can substitute canned jalapeño peppers for the mild green chilies or add 2 teaspoons of chipotle powder.

1. Add the beans and water to a container; cover, and let the beans soak 8 hours at room temperature.

2. Add the oil and the onion to the pressure cooker; sauté for 3 minutes or until the onion is soft. Add the garlic and sauté for 30 seconds.

3. Drain the beans and add them to the pressure cooker along with the tomatoes, chilies, chili powder, and oregano. Stir well. Lock the lid into place. Bring to high pressure; maintain pressure for 12 minutes. Remove from heat and allow pressure to release naturally for 10 minutes.

4. Quick-release any remaining pressure. Remove the lid. Transfer the cooked beans mixture to a food processor or blender. Add the cilantro and process until smooth. Taste for seasoning; add salt, to taste.

5. Transfer the dip to a bowl. Stir in the cheese. Serve warm.

Serves 12

1 cup dried black beans
2 cups water
1 tablespoon olive oil
1 small onion, diced
3 cloves garlic, minced
1 (14.5-ounce) can diced tomatoes
2 (4-ounce) cans mild green chilies, finely chopped
1 teaspoon chili powder
½ teaspoon dried oregano
¼ cup finely chopped fresh cilantro
Salt, to taste
1 cup vegan Monterey jack cheese, such as Follow Your Heart Vegan Gourmet Monterey Jack Cheese Alternative

---

🔥 OTHER BEAN OPTIONS

Bean dips are delicious when made with a variety of dried beans. To complement the flavors in this recipe, use black beans, pinto beans, or white beans. If you're pressed for time, use canned beans instead of dried beans, but be sure to drain the liquid first.

Tofu and Portobello Enchiladas

Turn up the heat by adding some fresh minced or canned chilies. If you're addicted to vegan cheese, add a handful of grated cheese to the filling as well as on top.

Serves 4

1 (16-ounce) block firm tofu, diced small
5 portobello mushrooms, chopped
1 onion, diced
3 cloves garlic, minced
2 tablespoons oil
2 teaspoons chili powder
½ cup sliced black olives
1 (15-ounce) can enchilada sauce, divided
8–10 flour tortillas
½ cup vegan cheese (optional)

1. Preheat oven to 350°F.

2. In a large skillet, heat the tofu, mushrooms, onion, and garlic in oil until tofu is just lightly sautéed, about 4–5 minutes. Add chili powder and heat for 1 more minute, stirring to coat well.

3. Remove from heat and add black olives and ⅓ cup enchilada sauce, and combine well.

4. Spread a thin layer of enchilada sauce in the bottom of a baking pan or casserole dish.

5. Place about ¼ cup of the tofu and mushrooms in each flour tortilla and roll, placing snugly in the baking dish. Top with remaining enchilada sauce, coating the tops of each tortilla well.

6. Sprinkle with vegan cheese if desired, and bake for 25–30 minutes.

🔥 VEGETABLE ENCHILADAS

Omit the mushrooms and grate a couple carrots and zucchinis to use in the filling instead. They'll bake quickly when grated, so no need to precook.

Portobello and Pepper Fajitas

Chopped seitan could take the place of the portobellos in these spicy fajitas if you prefer, or look for vegan "steak" or "chicken" strips.

1. Heat olive oil in a large skillet and add mushrooms, bell peppers, and onion. Allow to cook for 3–5 minutes until vegetables are almost done.

2. Add chili powder, cumin, and hot sauce, and stir to combine. Cook for 2–3 more minutes until mushrooms and peppers are soft. Remove from heat and stir in fresh cilantro.

3. Layer the vegetable mixture in flour tortillas and top with salsa, fresh sliced avocados, and/ or vegan sour cream.

Serves 4

2 tablespoons olive oil
2 large portobello mushrooms, cut into strips
1 green bell pepper, cut into strips
1 red bell pepper, cut into strips
1 onion, cut into strips
¾ teaspoon chili powder
¼ teaspoon cumin
Dash hot sauce
1 tablespoon chopped fresh cilantro
4 flour tortillas, warmed
Toppings: salsa, sliced avocados, vegan sour cream, etc.

Chickpea Soft Tacos

For an easy and healthy taco filling wrapped up in flour tortillas, try using chickpeas! Short on time? Pick up taco seasoning packets to use instead of the spice blend—but know that the dish might not be as spicy.

Serves 6

2 (15-ounce) cans chickpeas, drained
½ cup water
1 (6-ounce) can tomato paste
1 tablespoon chili powder
1 teaspoon garlic powder
½ teaspoon onion powder
½ teaspoon cumin
¼ cup chopped fresh cilantro (optional)
4 flour tortillas
Optional taco toppings: shredded lettuce, black olives, vegan cheese, nondairy sour cream

1. Combine chickpeas, water, tomato paste, chili, garlic, and onion powders, and cumin in a large skillet. Cover, and simmer for 10 minutes, stirring occasionally. Uncover, and simmer another 1–2 minutes until most of the liquid is absorbed.

2. Uncover, and use a fork or potato masher to mash the chickpeas until half mashed. Stir in fresh cilantro if desired.

3. Spoon mixture into flour tortillas, add toppings, and wrap.

Southwest Sweet Potato Enchiladas

These hot and spicy enchiladas freeze well, so make a double batch and thaw and reheat when you're hungry!

1. Preheat oven to 350°F.

2. In a large bowl, combine the sweet potatoes, onion, garlic, beans, lime juice, chilies, chili powder, and cumin until well mixed.

3. In a separate bowl, combine the enchilada sauce and water. Add ¼ cup of this mixture to the beans and sweet potatoes and combine well.

4. Spread about ⅓ cup sauce in the bottom of a casserole or baking dish.

5. Place about ⅓ cup bean and potato mixture in each tortilla and wrap, then place in the casserole dish. Repeat until all filling is used.

6. Spread a generous layer of the remaining enchilada sauce over the top of the rolled tortillas, being sure to coat all the edges and corners well. You may have a little sauce left over.

7. Bake for 25–30 minutes. If enchiladas dry out while baking, top with more sauce.

Serves 4

2 medium sweet potatoes, baked and diced
½ onion, minced
3 cloves garlic, minced
1 (15-ounce) can black beans, drained
2 teaspoons lime juice
2 tablespoons sliced green chilies
2 teaspoons chili powder
1 teaspoon cumin
1 (15-ounce) can green chili enchilada sauce
½ cup water
10–12 corn tortillas, warmed

🔥 SWEET POTATO BURRITOS

Sweet potatoes and black beans make lovely vegan burritos as well as enchiladas. Omit the enchilada sauce and wrap the mixture in flour tortillas along with the usual taco fixings.

Caramelized Onion and Mushroom Cheeseless Quesadillas

Sure, you can easily make vegan quesadillas using vegan cheese, but try this more nutritious version filled with a cheesy bean spread.

Serves 6

½ onion, chopped
1 cup sliced mushrooms
½ cup chopped canned jalapeño slices
2 cloves garlic
2 tablespoons olive oil
Dash salt and pepper
1 (15-ounce) can white beans, any kind, drained
1 medium tomato
3 tablespoons nutritional yeast
3 tablespoons lemon juice
½ teaspoon cumin
6 flour tortillas
Oil for frying

1. Sauté onion, mushrooms, jalapeño, and garlic in olive oil in a large skillet and add a dash of salt and pepper. Cook, stirring occasionally, until onion and mushrooms are browned and caramelized, about 8 minutes.

2. In a food processor or blender, purée together the white beans, tomato, nutritional yeast, lemon juice, and cumin until smooth.

3. Spread ⅓ of the bean mixture on each of 3 tortillas, then top with a portion of the mushrooms and onions. Top with additional tortillas.

4. Lightly fry in oil for 2–3 minutes on each side, just until tortillas are lightly crispy.

CHAPTER 4

Soups, Stews, and Chilies

SOUPS

Vegetable Broth

Red Lentil Soup

Tortilla Soup

Black Bean Soup

Chinese Hot and Sour Soup

Cold Spanish Gazpacho with Avocado

Kidney Bean and Zucchini Gumbo

African Peanut and Greens Soup

Thai Tom Kha Kai Coconut Soup

STEWS

Jamaican Red Bean Stew

Étouffée

Gumbo z'Herbes

Korean-Style Hot Pot

Posole

Curried Seitan Stew

Succotash Stew

"Beef" and Barley Stew

CHILIES

Black Bean and Butternut Squash Chili

Black Bean, Corn, and Fresh Tomato Chili

Chili con "Carne"

Cincinnati Chili

Fajita Chili

Five-Pepper Chili

Lentil Chili

Pumpkin Chili

Red Bean Chili

Shredded "Chicken" Chili

Southwest Vegetable Chili

Red-Hot Summer Chili

Super "Meaty" Chili with TVP

Spicy Sweet Potato Chili

Ten-Minute Cheater's Chili

Three-Bean Chili

Barley and Bell Pepper Chili

Vegetable Broth

This versatile Vegetable Broth can be used as the base for almost any soup or stew. It's not really spicy, but it acts as a base for a variety of other fiery recipes.

Yields 4 cups

2 large onions, halved

2 medium carrots, cut into large pieces

3 stalks celery, cut in half

1 whole bulb garlic, crushed

10 peppercorns

1 bay leaf

6 cups water

1. In a 4-quart slow cooker, add all ingredients, cover, and cook on low heat for 8–10 hours.

2. Strain the Vegetable Broth to remove the vegetables. Store in the refrigerator.

 STORING BROTH

Homemade Vegetable Broth can be stored in a covered container in the refrigerator for 2–3 days, or frozen for up to 3 months.

Red Lentil Soup

This spicy soup is perfect for lunch or as a dinner starter. If you want to spice it up even more, just add more cayenne pepper!

1. In a sauté pan, heat the olive oil over medium heat, then sauté the onion, ginger, and garlic for 2–3 minutes.

2. In a 4-quart slow cooker, add the sautéed vegetables and all remaining ingredients, cover, and cook on low for 6–8 hours. Add more salt if necessary, to taste.

🔥 CLEANING LENTILS

Before cooking lentils, rinse them carefully by placing in a colander and running ample cold water over the lentils. Sort through the bunch to remove and discard any debris that may be lingering behind.

Serves 6

3 tablespoons olive oil
1 small onion, sliced
1½ teaspoons minced fresh ginger
2 cloves garlic, minced
2 cups red lentils
6 cups Vegetable Broth (see recipe in this chapter)
Juice of 1 lemon
½ teaspoon paprika
1 teaspoon cayenne pepper
1½ teaspoons salt

Tortilla Soup

Turn this spicy soup into a complete meal by adding pieces of cooked vegan chicken, such as Morningstar Farms Meal Starters Chik'n Strips or Gardein Seasoned Bites.

Serves 8

2 tablespoons olive oil
1 large onion, chopped
2 cloves garlic, minced
2 tablespoons soy sauce
7 cups Vegetable Broth (see recipe in this chapter)
1 (16-ounce) package firm silken tofu, crumbled
2 cups diced tomato
1 cup corn kernels
1 teaspoon chipotle powder
1 teaspoon cayenne pepper
2 teaspoons ground cumin
2 teaspoons salt
1 teaspoon dried oregano
10 small corn tortillas, sliced
1 (8-ounce) package shredded vegan cheese, such as Daiya Mozzarella Style Shreds

1. In a sauté pan over medium heat, add the olive oil; sauté the onion until just soft, about 3 minutes. Add the garlic and sauté for an additional 30 seconds.

2. In a 4-quart slow cooker, add all ingredients except tortillas and cheese. Stir, cover, and cook on low heat for 4 hours.

3. While the soup is cooking, preheat oven to 450°F. Slice the corn tortillas into thin strips and place them on an ungreased baking sheet. Bake for about 10 minutes, or until they turn golden brown. Remove from heat and set aside.

4. After the soup has cooled slightly, use an immersion blender or regular blender to purée the soup.

5. Serve with cooked tortilla strips and 1 ounce of shredded cheese in each bowl of soup.

🌶 CHIPOTLE POWDER

Chipotle powder is made from ground chipotle peppers, a type of dried jalapeño. They bring a smoky spiciness to dishes but can be replaced with cayenne pepper or chili powder.

Black Bean Soup

You can use the leftover red onion from this spicy recipe to make Fajita Chili (see recipe in this chapter).

1. In a sauté pan, heat the olive oil over medium heat, then sauté the bell peppers, onion, and garlic for 2–3 minutes.

2. In a 4-quart slow cooker, add the sautéed vegetables, black beans, cumin, chipotle powder, salt, and Vegetable Broth. Cover, and cook on low for 6 hours.

3. Let the soup cool slightly, then pour half into a blender. Process until smooth, then pour back into the pot. Add the chopped cilantro, and stir.

Serves 6

2 tablespoons olive oil
½ green bell pepper, diced
½ red bell pepper, diced
½ red onion, sliced
2 cloves garlic, minced
2 (15-ounce) cans black beans, drained and rinsed
2 teaspoons cumin seeds, minced
1 teaspoon chipotle powder
1 teaspoon salt
4 cups Vegetable Broth (see recipe in this chapter)
¼ cup chopped cilantro

Chinese Hot and Sour Soup

If this Americanized version of hot and sour soup just doesn't satisfy your Szechuan cravings, hit up a specialty Asian grocery store and replace the cabbage with ½ cup dried lily buds and substitute half of the shiitake with wood ear fungus.

Serves 6

2 cups seitan or other meat substitute, diced small
2 tablespoons vegetable oil
1½ teaspoons hot sauce
6 cups Vegetable Broth (see recipe in this chapter)
½ head Napa cabbage, shredded
¾ cup sliced shiitake mushrooms
1 small can bamboo shoots, drained
2 tablespoons soy sauce
2 tablespoons white vinegar
¾ teaspoon red pepper flakes
¾ teaspoon salt
2 tablespoons cornstarch
¼ cup water
3 scallions, sliced
2 teaspoons chili oil

1. Brown seitan in vegetable oil for 2–3 minutes until cooked. Reduce heat to low and add hot sauce, stirring well to coat. Cook over low heat for 1 more minute, then remove from heat and set aside.

2. In a large soup pot or stockpot, combine Vegetable Broth, cabbage, mushrooms, bamboo, soy sauce, vinegar, red pepper flakes, and salt. Bring to a slow simmer and cover. Simmer for at least 15 minutes.

3. In a separate small bowl, whisk together the cornstarch and water, then slowly stir into soup. Heat just until soup thickens.

4. Portion into serving bowl, then top each serving with scallions and drizzle with chili oil.

Cold Spanish Gazpacho with Avocado

This gazpacho is best enjoyed on an outdoor patio just after sunset on a warm summer evening. But really, anytime you want a simple, spicy starter soup, this will do, no matter the weather. Add some crunch by topping with homemade croutons.

1. Mix together the cucumbers, red onion, tomatoes, cilantro, and avocados. Set half of the mixture aside. Take the other half and mix in a blender. Add the garlic, lime juice, vinegar, Vegetable Broth, and chili pepper or hot sauce and process until smooth.

2. Transfer to serving bowl and add reserved cucumbers, onion, tomatoes, cilantro, and avocados, gently stirring to combine.

3. Season generously with salt and pepper, to taste.

Serves 6

2 cucumbers, diced
½ red onion, diced
2 large tomatoes, diced
¼ cup chopped fresh cilantro
2 avocados, diced
4 cloves garlic
2 tablespoons lime juice
1 tablespoon red wine vinegar
¾ cup Vegetable Broth (see recipe in this chapter)
1 chili pepper (jalapeño, serrano, or cayenne) or 1 teaspoon hot sauce
Salt and pepper, to taste

🔥 CRUNCHY CROUTONS

Slice your favorite vegan artisan bread, focaccia, or whatever you've got into 1" cubes. Toss them in a large bowl with a generous coating of olive oil or a flavored oil, a bit of salt, and some Italian seasoning, garlic powder, a dash of cayenne, or whatever you prefer, then transfer to a baking sheet and bake 15–20 minutes at 275°F, tossing once or twice.

Kidney Bean and Zucchini Gumbo

This vegetable gumbo uses zucchini instead of okra. Traditional gumbo always calls for filé powder, but if you can't find this anywhere, increase the amounts of the other spices—especially the Cajun seasoning—to give this dish even more of a kick!

Serves 5

1 onion, diced
1 red or green bell pepper, chopped
3 stalks celery, chopped
2 tablespoons olive oil
1 zucchini, sliced
1 (14-ounce) can diced tomatoes
3 cups Vegetable Broth (see recipe in this chapter)
1 teaspoon hot sauce
1 teaspoon filé powder (optional)
¾ teaspoon thyme
1 teaspoon Cajun seasoning
2 bay leaves
1 (15-ounce) can kidney beans, drained
1½ cups rice, cooked

1. In a large soup pot or stock pan, sauté the onion, bell pepper, and celery in olive oil for just 1–2 minutes. Reduce heat and add remaining ingredients except beans and rice.

2. Bring to a simmer, cover, and allow to cook for 30 minutes.

3. Uncover, add beans, and stir to combine. Heat for 5 more minutes. Remove bay leaves before serving. Serve over cooked rice.

🔥 GUMBO ON THE GO

If you don't have some precooked rice on hand, add ⅔ cup instant rice and an extra cup of Vegetable Broth during the last 10 minutes of cooking. For a "meatier texture," quickly brown some vegan sausage or ground beef substitute and toss it in the mix.

African Peanut and Greens Soup

Reduce the liquids in this soup to turn it into a thick and chunky curry to pour over rice. Although the ingredients are all familiar, this is definitely not a boring meal!

1. In large pot, sauté the onion and tomatoes in olive oil until onion is soft, about 2–3 minutes.

2. Reduce heat to medium-low and add remaining ingredients except spinach, stirring well to combine.

3. Allow to simmer on low heat, uncovered, stirring occasionally for 8–10 minutes.

4. Add spinach and allow to cook for another 1–2 minutes, just until spinach is wilted.

5. Remove from heat and adjust seasonings, to taste. Soup will thicken as it cools.

Serves 4

1 onion, diced
3 tomatoes, chopped
2 tablespoons olive oil
2 cups Vegetable Broth (see recipe in this chapter)
1 cup coconut milk
⅓ cup peanut butter
1 (15-ounce) can chickpeas, drained
½ teaspoon salt
1 teaspoon curry powder
1 teaspoon sugar
⅓ teaspoon red pepper flakes
1 bunch fresh spinach

Thai Tom Kha Kai Coconut Soup

In Thailand, this spicy soup is a full meal, served alongside a large plate of steamed rice, and the vegetables vary with the season and whim of the chef—broccoli, bell peppers, or mild chilies are common. Don't worry if you can't find lemongrass or galangal, as lime and ginger add a similar flavor.

Serves 4

1 (14-ounce) can coconut milk
2 cups Vegetable Broth (see recipe in this chapter)
1 tablespoon soy sauce
3 cloves garlic, minced
5 slices fresh ginger or galangal
1 stalk lemongrass, chopped (optional)
1 tablespoon lime juice
1–2 small chilies, chopped
½ teaspoon red pepper flakes, or to taste
1 onion, chopped
2 tomatoes, chopped
1 carrot, sliced thin
½ cup sliced mushrooms, any kind
¼ cup chopped fresh cilantro

1. In large pot, combine the coconut milk and Vegetable Broth over low heat. Add soy sauce, garlic, ginger or galangal, lemongrass if desired, lime juice, chilies, and red pepper flakes. Heat, but do not boil.

2. When Vegetable Broth is hot, add onion, tomatoes, carrot, and mushrooms. Cover, and cook on low heat for 10–15 minutes.

3. Remove from heat and top with chopped fresh cilantro.

Jamaican Red Bean Stew

Make your own hot and spicy jerk seasoning by combining thyme, allspice, black pepper, cinnamon, cayenne, onion powder, and nutmeg.

1. In a sauté pan over medium heat, add the
olive oil, then sauté the onion and garlic for
about 3 minutes.

2. In a 4-quart slow cooker, add all ingredients.
Cover, and cook on low heat for 6 hours.

Serves 4

2 tablespoons olive oil
½ onion, diced
2 cloves garlic, minced
1 (15-ounce) can diced
   tomatoes
3 cups peeled and diced sweet
   potatoes
2 (15-ounce) cans red kidney
   beans, drained
1 cup coconut milk
3 cups Vegetable Broth (see
   recipe in this chapter)
2 teaspoons jerk seasoning
2 teaspoons curry powder
Salt and pepper, to taste

Étouffée

You can purchase the vegan shrimp used in this spicy dish online at VeganStore.com.

Serves 6

½ cup vegan margarine
1 onion, diced
3 celery ribs, chopped
1 carrot, diced
3 cloves garlic, minced
1 green bell pepper, chopped
¼ cup flour
1 cup water
2 teaspoons Cajun seasoning
1 (8.8-ounce) package vegan
   shrimp
Juice of 1 lemon
½ teaspoon salt
¼ teaspoon black pepper
4 cups cooked white rice
½ cup chopped parsley

1. In a sauté pan over medium heat, add the vegan margarine. Sauté the onion, celery, carrot, garlic, and green bell pepper until soft, about 5–7 minutes. Stir in the flour to make a roux.

2. Add the roux to a 4-quart slow cooker. Whisk in the water, Cajun seasoning, vegan shrimp, lemon juice, salt, and pepper. Cover, and cook on low heat for 4–5 hours.

3. Serve over the white rice and garnish with parsley.

 CAJUN SEASONING

To make your own Cajun seasoning, use a blend of equal parts cayenne pepper, black pepper, paprika, garlic powder, onion powder, salt, and thyme.

Gumbo z'Herbes

You won't miss the meat with all the delicious flavors in this gumbo. As they say in New Orleans, *"Laissez les bons temps rouler!"* Or, "Let the good times roll!"

1. Add the olive oil to the slow cooker and sauté the onion, bell pepper, and celery on low heat for 4–5 minutes. Add the garlic and sauté for 1 minute more.

2. Slowly whisk in the flour to create a roux. Pour in the Vegetable Broth and continue to whisk to remove all lumps.

3. Add the rest of the ingredients except the rice and cook on high heat for 3–4 hours. Serve over the cooked white rice.

Serves 6

½ cup olive oil
1 onion, chopped
1 green bell pepper, chopped
2 stalks celery, chopped
4 cloves garlic, minced
½ cup flour
4 cups Vegetable Broth (see recipe in this chapter)
2 cups okra, chopped
½ teaspoon dried thyme
½ teaspoon dried oregano
1 teaspoon salt
½ teaspoon black pepper
¼ teaspoon red pepper flakes
6 cups cooked white rice

♨ THE HOLY TRINITY

The base of some of New Orleans's most well-known dishes is referred to as the "holy trinity." It contains equal parts onions, bell pepper, and celery.

Korean-Style Hot Pot

Serve this hot and spicy main dish with sides of steamed rice and kimchi (a side of fermented vegetables).

Serves 8

3 bunches baby bok choy
8 cups water
8 ounces sliced cremini mushrooms
1 (16-ounce) package extra-firm tofu, cubed
3 cloves garlic, thinly sliced
¼ teaspoon sesame oil
1 tablespoon red pepper flakes
7 ounces enoki mushrooms

1. Remove the leaves of the baby bok choy. Wash thoroughly.

2. Place the leaves whole in a 4-quart slow cooker. Add the water, cremini mushrooms, tofu, garlic, sesame oil, and red pepper flakes. Stir.

3. Cook on low for 8 hours.

4. Add the enoki mushrooms and stir. Cook an additional ½ hour. Remove from heat and enjoy.

Posole

This rich-tasting, spicy stew just needs a sprinkling of shredded red cabbage to finish it to perfection.

1. Seed the chilies, reserving the seeds.

2. In a dry, hot frying pan, heat the chilies until warmed through and fragrant, about 2–3 minutes. Do not burn or brown them.

3. In a medium pot, place the chilies and seeds, 1 quart Vegetable Broth, garlic, lime juice, cumin, and oregano. Bring to a boil and continue to boil for 20 minutes.

4. Meanwhile, in a plastic bag, toss the Gardein Chick'n Strips with the flour to coat. Heat the oil in a large nonstick skillet and brown the vegan meat on all sides, about 3 minutes.

5. Add the onion and cook about 5 minutes, or until the onion is soft.

6. In a 4-quart slow cooker, pour ½ quart Vegetable Broth, hominy, and the onion and vegan meat mixture.

7. Strain the chili-stock mixture through a mesh sieve into the slow cooker insert, mashing down with a wooden spoon to press out the pulp and juice. Discard the seeds and remaining solids. Cook on low for 8 hours.

Serves 6

8 large dried New Mexican red chilies
1½ quarts Vegetable Broth (see recipe in this chapter), divided
3 cloves garlic, minced
2 tablespoons lime juice
1 tablespoon ground cumin
1 tablespoon oregano
1 (7-ounce) package Gardein Chick'n Strips
¾ cup flour
1 teaspoon canola oil
1 large onion, sliced
1 (40-ounce) can hominy

Curried Seitan Stew

Adding a small amount of soy sauce to a curry dish gives it a richness that is normally achieved with fish sauce in recipes that aren't vegan.

Serves 4

2 tablespoons olive oil
½ onion, chopped
2 cloves garlic, minced
1 teaspoon minced fresh ginger
2 tablespoons panang curry paste
1 teaspoon paprika
1 teaspoon sugar
½ teaspoon cayenne pepper
1 teaspoon soy sauce
1 (14-ounce) can coconut milk
3 cups Vegetable Broth (see recipe in this chapter)
2 cups cubed seitan
½ teaspoon salt
¼ teaspoon pepper
¼ cup chopped cilantro

1. In a 4-quart slow cooker, add all ingredients except the cilantro. Cover, and cook on low heat for 4 hours.

2. Garnish with cilantro before serving.

Succotash Stew

Try adding chopped okra to this versatile southern stew.

1. Place the dry lima beans and 7 cups water in a 4-quart slow cooker, cover, and cook on high heat for 4 hours. Drain the lima beans.

2. Place the drained lima beans, 1 cup water, corn, tomatoes, bay leaves, thyme, oregano, cayenne pepper, salt, and black pepper in the slow cooker and cook on low heat for 4 hours.

Serves 6

1 pound dry lima beans
8 cups water, divided
2 (14-ounce) cans corn, drained
2 (14-ounce) cans diced
    tomatoes
2 bay leaves
1 teaspoon dried thyme
1 teaspoon dried oregano
1 teaspoon cayenne pepper
¼ teaspoon salt
⅛ teaspoon black pepper

"Beef" and Barley Stew

Classic and comforting, you can't go wrong with this spicy "beef" and barley stew on a cold night.

Serves 6

1 onion, chopped
2 ribs celery, chopped
1 carrot, chopped
1 green bell pepper, chopped
2 tablespoons olive oil
1 cup water
2½ cups tomato or mixed
  vegetable juice
⅓ cup barley
1½ teaspoons chili powder
1½ teaspoons parsley or Italian
  seasoning
2 bay leaves
4 veggie burgers, crumbled
Salt and pepper, to taste

1. Heat the onion, celery, carrot, and bell pepper in olive oil in a large soup pot or stockpot, just until veggies are almost soft, about 4–5 minutes.

2. Add water, tomato or vegetable juice, and barley, stirring well to combine, then add chili powder, parsley or Italian seasoning, and bay leaves.

3. Cover, and cook over medium-low heat for 20 minutes. Add veggie burgers and cook for another 5 minutes, uncovered, or until barley is soft.

4. Season with salt and pepper, to taste; remove bay leaves before serving.

🌶 BEAN AND BARLEY STEW

TVP or a store-bought meat substitute could work in this stew, but the chewiness of the veggie burgers provides a nice complement to the equally chewy barley. If you don't have any of these on hand, add some beans instead for a thick and hearty meal.

Black Bean and Butternut Squash Chili

Squash is an excellent addition to vegan chili in this hot and spicy southwestern-style dish.

1. In a large stockpot, sauté onion and garlic in oil until soft, about 4 minutes.

2. Reduce heat and add remaining ingredients except cilantro.

3. Cover, and simmer for 25 minutes. Uncover, and simmer another 5 minutes. Top with fresh cilantro if desired just before serving.

Serves 4

1 onion, chopped
3 cloves garlic, minced
2 tablespoons oil
1 medium butternut squash, chopped into chunks
2 (15-ounce) cans black beans, drained
1 (28-ounce) can stewed or diced tomatoes, undrained
¾ cup water or Vegetable Broth (see recipe in this chapter)
1 tablespoon chili powder
1 teaspoon cumin
¼ teaspoon cayenne pepper, or to taste
½ teaspoon salt
2 tablespoons chopped fresh cilantro (optional)

Black Bean, Corn, and Fresh Tomato Chili

Tofutti makes a delicious nondairy sour cream called Sour Supreme, and it can be found in some national grocery store chains. Use it to garnish this deliciously spicy dish!

Serves 4

1 red onion, diced
1 jalapeño, seeded and minced
3 cloves garlic, minced
1 (15-ounce) can black beans, drained
1 (15-ounce) can corn, drained
3 tablespoons chili powder
1 tablespoon paprika
1 teaspoon dried oregano
1 teaspoon ground cumin
½ teaspoon chipotle powder
2 cups Vegetable Broth (see recipe in this chapter)
½ teaspoon salt
¼ teaspoon black pepper
2 cups diced tomatoes
¼ cup chopped cilantro
4 tablespoons vegan sour cream

1. In a 4-quart slow cooker, add all ingredients except tomatoes, cilantro, and sour cream. Cover, and cook on low heat for 5 hours.

2. When the chili is done cooking, mix in the tomatoes and garnish with the cilantro. Top with vegan sour cream.

Chili con "Carne"

Try Boca Ground Crumbles in this fast and fiery recipe as a vegan alternative to ground beef.

In a 4-quart slow cooker, add all ingredients. Cover, and cook on low heat for 5 hours.

🔥 VEGAN BEEF

In addition to Boca Ground Crumbles, there are other types of vegan ground beef on the market. Try Gimme Lean Ground Beef Style, Match Ground Beef, or TVP.

Serves 4

½ cup diced onion
½ cup diced bell pepper
1 (12-ounce) package frozen
    veggie burger crumbles
2 cloves garlic, minced
1 (15-ounce) can kidney beans,
    rinsed and drained
2 cups Vegetable Broth (see
    recipe in this chapter)
1 tablespoon chili powder
½ tablespoon chipotle powder
½ tablespoon cumin
1 teaspoon thyme
1 tablespoon oregano
2 cups diced fresh tomatoes
1 tablespoon tomato paste
1 tablespoon cider vinegar
1 teaspoon salt

Cincinnati Chili

Cincinnati chili is native to the state of Ohio and is typically served over spaghetti or on hot dogs.

Serves 4

1 onion, chopped
1 (12-ounce) package frozen
    veggie burger crumbles
3 cloves garlic, minced
1 cup tomato sauce
1 cup water
2 tablespoons red wine vinegar
2 tablespoons chili powder
½ teaspoon cumin
½ teaspoon ground cinnamon
½ teaspoon paprika
½ teaspoon ground allspice
1 tablespoon light brown sugar
1 tablespoon unsweetened
    cocoa powder
1 teaspoon hot sauce
1 (16-ounce) package spaghetti,
    cooked
Vegan cheese (optional)
Additional chopped onion for
    topping (optional)
Pinto beans (optional)

1. In a 4-quart slow cooker, add all ingredients except the spaghetti and optional ingredients. Cover, and cook on low heat for 5 hours.

2. Serve the chili over the spaghetti and top with vegan cheese, onions, and/or pinto beans if desired.

🔥 WAYS TO SERVE

Cincinnati chili is known for being served up to five ways: two-way means chili and spaghetti; three-way means chili, spaghetti, and vegan Cheddar cheese; four-way means chili, spaghetti, vegan cheese, and onions or pinto beans; and five-way means all of the above!

Fajita Chili

Re-create the flavor of sizzling, spicy restaurant faji-tas in your own home!

In a 4-quart slow cooker, add all ingredients. Cover, and cook on low heat for 5 hours.

🌶 SIMPLIFY THIS RECIPE

One way to simplify this recipe is to use a packet of fajita seasoning (sold in the international aisle in many stores) in place of the chili powder, sugar, paprika, garlic powder, cayenne pepper, cumin, salt, and black pepper.

Serves 6

1 red onion, diced
1 jalapeño, seeded and minced
3 cloves garlic, minced
1 (15-ounce) can black beans, drained
1 (15-ounce) can diced toma-toes, drained
1 (7-ounce) package Gardein Chick'n Strips, cut into bite-size pieces
2 cups Vegetable Broth (see recipe in this chapter)
2 teaspoons chili powder
1 teaspoon sugar
1 teaspoon paprika
¼ teaspoon garlic powder
¼ teaspoon cayenne pepper
¼ teaspoon cumin
1 teaspoon salt
¼ teaspoon black pepper

Five-Pepper Chili

Sound the alarm! This blazing-hot chili will set your mouth afire!

Serves 8

1 onion, diced
1 jalapeño, seeded and minced
1 habanero pepper, seeded and minced
1 bell pepper, diced
1 poblano pepper, seeded and diced
2 cloves garlic, minced
2 (15-ounce) cans crushed tomatoes
2 cups diced fresh tomatoes
2 tablespoons chili powder
1 tablespoon cumin
½ tablespoon cayenne pepper
⅛ cup vegan Worcestershire sauce
2 (15-ounce) cans pinto beans
1 teaspoon salt
¼ teaspoon black pepper

In a 4-quart slow cooker, add all ingredients. Cover, and cook on low heat for 5 hours.

Lentil Chili

Before using dried lentils in this spicy dish, rinse
them well and pick through to remove any debris or
undesirable pieces.

In a 4-quart slow cooker, add all ingredients.
Cover, and cook on low heat for 8 hours.

Serves 6

1 cup uncooked lentils

1 onion, diced

3 cloves garlic, minced

4 cups Vegetable Broth (see
recipe in this chapter)

¼ cup tomato paste

1 cup chopped carrots

1 cup chopped celery

1 (15-ounce) can diced tomatoes, drained

2 tablespoons chili powder

½ tablespoon paprika

1 teaspoon dried oregano

1 teaspoon cumin

1 teaspoon salt

¼ teaspoon black pepper

Pumpkin Chili

Pumpkin is typically complemented by sugar, cinnamon, and other earthy spices, but you'll see that it's delicious with a dash of heat, like chili powder.

Serves 6

2 tablespoons olive oil
1 onion, diced
2 (14-ounce) cans tomatoes
1 cup Vegetable Broth (see
    recipe in this chapter)
1 medium pumpkin, rind and
    seeds removed, flesh cut into
    ½" chunks
1 (14-ounce) can white beans,
    drained
2 tablespoons chili powder
3 teaspoons cumin
1 teaspoon salt
½ teaspoon black pepper

1. Add the oil to the slow cooker and sauté the onion on high heat for 3–5 minutes.

2. Add the rest of the ingredients and cook on low heat for 6 hours.

Red Bean Chili

In the United States, "red beans" most commonly refers to kidney beans, which add some meatiness to this red-hot dish.

In a 4-quart slow cooker, add all ingredients. Cover, and cook on low heat for 5 hours.

🔥 THE BENEFITS OF CANNED TOMATOES

In addition to being inexpensive and always available, canned tomatoes are higher in lycopene than fresh tomatoes, making them a great option for chili and stews.

Serves 4

2 (15-ounce) cans red kidney beans, drained
½ cup diced onion
2 cloves garlic, minced
2 cups Vegetable Broth (see recipe in this chapter)
1 tablespoon chili powder
½ tablespoon chipotle powder
½ tablespoon cumin
½ tablespoon paprika
1 (15-ounce) can diced tomatoes
½ teaspoon salt
¼ teaspoon black pepper

Shredded "Chicken" Chili

There are many vegan chicken substitutes on the market, but you can also use shredded seitan to replace the meat commonly found in this spicy dish.

Serves 4

½ cup diced onion
½ cup diced bell pepper
1 (7-ounce) package Gardein Chick'n Strips, shredded by hand
2 cloves garlic, minced
1 (15-ounce) can kidney beans, rinsed and drained
2 cups Vegetable Broth (see recipe in this chapter)
1 tablespoon chili powder
½ tablespoon chipotle powder
½ tablespoon cumin
1 teaspoon thyme
1 tablespoon oregano
1 (15-ounce) can diced tomatoes, drained
1 tablespoon tomato paste
1 tablespoon cider vinegar
1 teaspoon salt

In a 4-quart slow cooker, add all ingredients. Cover, and cook on low heat for 5 hours.

Southwest Vegetable Chili

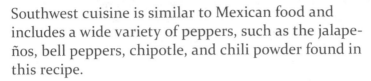

Southwest cuisine is similar to Mexican food and includes a wide variety of peppers, such as the jalapeños, bell peppers, chipotle, and chili powder found in this recipe.

In a 4-quart slow cooker, add all ingredients. Cover, and cook on low heat for 5 hours.

Serves 4

1 (28-ounce) can diced tomatoes
1 (15-ounce) can red kidney beans
1 onion, chopped
1 green bell pepper, chopped
1 red bell pepper, chopped
1 zucchini, chopped
1 squash, chopped
¼ cup pickled jalapeños, chopped
⅛ cup chili powder
2 tablespoons garlic powder
2 tablespoons cumin
1 teaspoon chipotle powder
⅛ teaspoon dried thyme
¼ teaspoon black pepper

Red-Hot Summer Chili

This hot and spicy chili is full of summer vegetables, and you can add vegan chicken for a heartier dish.

Serves 8

1 bulb fennel, diced
4 radishes, diced
2 stalks celery including leaves, diced
2 carrots, cut into coin-size pieces
1 medium onion, diced
1 shallot, diced
4 cloves garlic, sliced
1 habanero pepper, diced
1 (15-ounce) can cannellini beans, drained and rinsed
1 (12-ounce) can tomato paste
½ teaspoon dried oregano
½ teaspoon black pepper
½ teaspoon crushed rosemary
½ teaspoon cayenne pepper
½ teaspoon ground chipotle
1 teaspoon chili powder
1 teaspoon tarragon
¼ teaspoon cumin
¼ teaspoon celery seed
2 zucchinis, cubed
10 campari tomatoes, quartered
1 cup corn kernels

1. In a 4-quart slow cooker, add the fennel, radishes, celery, carrots, onion, shallot, garlic, habanero, beans, tomato paste, and all spices; stir. Cook on low for 6–7 hours.

2. Stir in the zucchinis, tomatoes, and corn. Cook for an additional 30 minutes on high. Stir before serving.

🔥 CAMPARI TOMATOES

Campari is a variety of tomato that is grown on the vine and has a sweet, juicy taste. It is round and on the small side, but not as small as a cherry tomato.

Super "Meaty" Chili with TVP

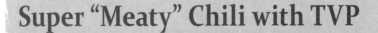

Any mock meat will work well in a vegan chili, but TVP is easy to keep on hand and very inexpensive. This is more of a thick, "meaty," Texas-style chili than a vegetable chili, but chili is easy and forgiving, so if you want to toss in some zucchini, broccoli, diced carrots, or even add an additional jalapeño pepper, by all means, do!

1. Cover the TVP with hot Vegetable Broth and soy sauce. Allow to sit for 3–4 minutes only, then drain.

2. In a large soup pot or stockpot, sauté the onion and garlic in olive oil until onion is soft, about 3–4 minutes.

3. Add remaining ingredients and TVP, stirring well to combine. Cover, and allow to simmer over low heat for at least 30 minutes, stirring occasionally.

4. Adjust seasonings, to taste.

🔥 REHYDRATING TVP

Most of the time, TVP needs to be rehydrated in hot water for 8–10 minutes in order to be fully rehydrated, unless it will be hydrated when cooking, such as in a soup with extra liquid. But the secret in this recipe is to only partially rehydrate the TVP, so that it absorbs some of the spices from the chili and the liquid from the tomatoes.

Serves 6

1½ cups TVP granules
1 cup hot Vegetable Broth (see recipe in this chapter)
1 tablespoon soy sauce
1 yellow onion, chopped
5 cloves garlic, minced
2 tablespoons olive oil
1 cup corn kernels (fresh, frozen, or canned)
1 bell pepper, any color, chopped
2 (15-ounce) cans beans (black, kidney, or pinto)
1 (15-ounce) can diced tomatoes
1 jalapeño pepper, minced, or ½ teaspoon cayenne pepper (optional)
1 teaspoon cumin
2 tablespoons chili powder
Salt and pepper, to taste

Spicy Sweet Potato Chili

Sweet potatoes are great sources of fiber and beta carotene, making this hot chili healthy and delicious.

Serves 4

1 red onion, diced
1 jalapeño, seeded and minced
3 cloves garlic, minced
1 (15-ounce) can black beans, drained
1 sweet potato, peeled and diced
3 tablespoons chili powder
1 tablespoon paprika
1 teaspoon dried oregano
1 teaspoon ground cumin
½ teaspoon chipotle powder
1 (28-ounce) can diced tomatoes, drained
2 cups Vegetable Broth (see recipe in this chapter)
¼ teaspoon black pepper
Juice of 1 lime
¼ cup chopped cilantro

1. In a 4-quart slow cooker, add all ingredients except the lime and cilantro. Cover, and cook on low heat for 8 hours.

2. When the chili is done cooking, mix in the lime juice and garnish with the cilantro.

🔥 WHAT IS CHILI POWDER?

Chili powder is made from grinding dried chilies, and may be created from a blend of different types of chilies or just one variety. The most commonly used chilies are red peppers and cayenne peppers.

Ten-Minute Cheater's Chili

No time? No problem! This spicy chili gives you a quick and easy way to get some veggies and protein on the table with no hassle. Instead of veggie burgers, you could toss in a handful of TVP flakes if you'd like, or any other mock meat you happen to have on hand.

In a large pot, combine all ingredients. Simmer for 10 minutes, stirring frequently.

Serves 4

1 (12-ounce) jar salsa

1 (14-ounce) can diced tomatoes

2 (14-ounce) cans kidney beans or black beans, drained

1½ cups frozen veggies

4 veggie burgers, crumbled (optional)

2 tablespoons chili powder

1 teaspoon cumin

½ cup water

Three-Bean Chili

Using dried beans will save you a little money on this spicy recipe, but be sure to soak the beans overnight to save on cooking time.

Serves 8

1 (15-ounce) can pinto beans, drained

1 (15-ounce) can black beans, drained

1 (15-ounce) can great northern white beans, drained

1 onion, diced

3 cloves garlic, minced

3 cups Vegetable Broth (see recipe in this chapter)

1 tablespoon chili powder

½ tablespoon chipotle powder

½ tablespoon cumin

½ tablespoon paprika

1 (15-ounce) can diced tomatoes

¼ teaspoon black pepper

In a 4-quart slow cooker, add all ingredients. Cover, and cook on low heat for 5 hours.

Barley and Bell Pepper Chili

With all the flavors and ingredients of traditional vegan chili, this recipe adds just a bit of whole-grain goodness to the mix.

1. In a large stockpot, heat the garlic, onion, and bell peppers in olive oil for 2–3 minutes. Add barley and toast, stirring frequently, for just 1 minute.

2. Reduce heat to medium-low and add water or Vegetable Broth, tomatoes, beans, chili powder, cumin, and oregano. Bring to a slow simmer, cover, and heat for at least 35 minutes, stirring occasionally.

3. Uncover, and adjust seasonings, to taste, then top with fresh chopped cilantro if desired.

🔥 WHOLE-GRAIN CHILI

Tossing in some cooked whole grains is a great way to stretch out your leftover chili, or just to add some healthy fiber and a touch of homemade goodness to canned chili or even canned baked beans. Although barley has a great texture for pairing with beans, leftover quinoa or millet would also work.

Serves 6

3 cloves garlic, minced
1 onion, chopped
1 green bell pepper, chopped
1 red bell pepper, chopped
2 tablespoons olive oil
½ cup barley
2½ cups water or Vegetable Broth (see recipe in this chapter)
1 (15-ounce) can diced tomatoes
1 (15-ounce) can black beans or kidney beans
2 tablespoons chili powder
1 teaspoon cumin
½ teaspoon oregano
2 tablespoons fresh chopped cilantro (optional)

CHAPTER 5

Vegetables, Stir-Fries, and Sides

Maple-Glazed Roast Veggies

Moroccan Root Vegetables

Ratatouille

Saucy Vaishnava Veggies

Marinated Artichokes

Baby Bok Choy

Cajun Collard Greens

Chipotle Corn on the Cob

Cilantro-Lime Corn on the Cob

Coconut Cauliflower Curry

Spicy Creamed Spinach

Spicy Turnip Greens

Black and Green Veggie Burritos

Fiery Basil and Eggplant Stir-Fry

Eggplant Caponata

Spicy "Baked" Eggplant

Garlic and Gingered Green Beans

Warm Jicama Slaw

Mango and Bell Pepper Stir-Fry

Stuffed Bell Peppers

Mexican Spice Potatoes

Potato Messaround

Potatoes Paprikash

Potato and Veggie Fritters

Cilantro Potato and Pea Curry

Southwestern Casserole

Polenta and Chili Casserole

Lime-Soaked Poblanos

Spicy Chipotle and Thyme Mashed Sweet Potatoes

Baked Sweet Potato Fries

Spicy Summer Squash Sauté

Maple-Glazed Roast Veggies

These easy roast veggies make an excellent spicy side dish. The vegetables can be roasted in advance and reheated with the glaze to save on time if needed. If parsnips are too earthy for you, substitute one large potato.

Serves 4

3 carrots, chopped
2 small parsnips, chopped
2 sweet potatoes, chopped
2 tablespoons olive oil
Salt and pepper, to taste
⅓ cup maple syrup
2 tablespoons Dijon mustard
1 tablespoon balsamic vinegar
1 teaspoon hot sauce

1. Preheat oven to 400°F.

2. On a large baking sheet, spread out chopped carrots, parsnips, and sweet potatoes. Drizzle with olive oil and season generously with salt and pepper. Roast for 40 minutes, tossing once.

3. In a small bowl, whisk together maple syrup, Dijon mustard, balsamic vinegar, and hot sauce.

4. Transfer the roasted vegetables to a large bowl and toss well with the maple syrup mixture. Add more salt and pepper, to taste.

🔥 SWEET AND SPICY GLAZE

This tangy and sweet glaze will lend itself well to a variety of roasted vegetables and combinations. Try it with roasted Brussels sprouts, beets, baby new potatoes, butternut or acorn squash, or even with roasted turnips or daikon radish.

Moroccan Root Vegetables

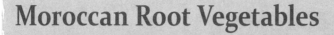

The Moroccan Root Vegetables recipe is good served with couscous and a yogurt or vegan side salad.

1. Add the parsnips, turnips, onions, carrots, apricots, prunes, turmeric, cumin, ginger, cinnamon, cayenne pepper, parsley, and cilantro to a 4-quart slow cooker.

2. Pour in the Vegetable Broth and salt.

3. Cover, and cook on low for 9 hours, or until the vegetables are cooked through.

Serves 8

1 pound parsnips, peeled and diced
1 pound turnips, peeled and diced
2 medium onions, chopped
1 pound carrots, peeled and diced
6 dried apricots, chopped
4 pitted prunes, chopped
1 teaspoon ground turmeric
1 teaspoon ground cumin
½ teaspoon ground ginger
½ teaspoon ground cinnamon
¼ teaspoon ground cayenne pepper
1 tablespoon dried parsley
1 tablespoon dried cilantro
2 cups Vegetable Broth (see Chapter 4)
1 teaspoon salt

Ratatouille

This spicy Ratatouille made in the slow cooker comes out surprisingly crisp-tender.

Serves 4

1 onion, roughly chopped
1 eggplant, sliced horizontally
2 zucchinis, sliced
1 cubanelle pepper, sliced
3 tomatoes, cut into wedges
2 tablespoons minced fresh basil
2 tablespoons minced fresh Italian parsley
¼ teaspoon salt
½ teaspoon freshly ground black pepper
3 ounces tomato paste
¼ cup water

1. Place the onion, eggplant, zucchinis, pepper, and tomatoes into a 4-quart slow cooker. Sprinkle with basil, parsley, salt, and pepper.

2. In a small bowl, whisk the tomato paste and water together. Pour the mixture over the vegetables. Stir.

3. Cook on low for 4 hours, or until the eggplant and zucchinis are fork-tender.

♨ CUBANELLE PEPPERS

Cubanelles look very similar to banana peppers and are similar in taste and heat, but they are two different varieties. Cubanelles can be mild to somewhat spicy and, like banana peppers, are often pickled.

Saucy Vaishnava Veggies

These simple, low-fat veggies will fill your kitchen with the smells and dreams of India as they simmer. Why not pick up a Bollywood movie to accompany your dinner?

1. Combine the tomatoes, potatoes, chili powder, curry powder, cumin, and turmeric in a large pot. Cover, and cook for 10 minutes.

2. Add chopped cauliflower, carrot, green peas, and red pepper flakes and cook, covered, for 15 more minutes until potatoes and vegetables are soft, stirring occasionally.

3. Season with salt, to taste.

Serves 4

1 (28-ounce) can diced tomatoes, undrained
2 potatoes, chopped small
½ teaspoon chili powder
2 teaspoons curry powder
1½ teaspoons cumin
½ teaspoon turmeric
1 head cauliflower, chopped
1 carrot, diced
¾ cup green peas
¾ teaspoon red pepper flakes
¼ teaspoon salt, or to taste

🔥 INDIAN VEGAN OPTIONS

In India, many vegetarians forswear eggs as well as onions and garlic for religious purposes, making Indian food an excellent choice for vegans. When eating at Indian restaurants, be sure to ask about ghee (Indian butter), which is a traditional ingredient, but easily and frequently substituted for with oil.

Marinated Artichokes

The marinated artichokes can be stored in the refrigerator for about a week, or if you jar them, about two months.

Serves 4

2 (9-ounce) boxes fresh artichoke hearts
½ cup olive oil
¼ cup apple cider vinegar
2 tablespoons lemon juice
3 bay leaves
1 teaspoon dried oregano
½ teaspoon salt
½ teaspoon red pepper flakes

Combine all ingredients in a 2-quart slow cooker and stir well. Cover, and cook on low heat for 2 hours.

Baby Bok Choy

Dark, leafy bok choy is a highly nutritious vegetable that can be found in well-stocked groceries. Keep an eye out for light green baby bok choy, which is a bit more tender but carries a similar flavor.

1. In a small bowl, whisk together all ingredients except the bok choy.

2. Place the bok choy in a 4-quart slow cooker and pour the soy sauce mixture over the bok choy. Cover, and cook on low heat for 3 hours.

Serves 6

2 tablespoons soy sauce
2 tablespoons apple cider vinegar
2 tablespoons sesame oil
½ teaspoon garlic powder
1 teaspoon red pepper flakes
3 heads baby bok choy, halved lengthwise

Cajun Collard Greens

Like Brussels sprouts and kimchi, collard greens are one of those foods folks tend to either love or hate. They're highly nutritious, so hopefully this hot and spicy recipe will turn you into a lover if you're not already.

Serves 4

1 onion, diced
3 cloves garlic, minced
1 pound collard greens, chopped
2 tablespoons olive oil
¾ cup water or Vegetable Broth (see Chapter 4)
1 (14-ounce) can diced tomatoes, drained
1½ teaspoons Cajun seasoning
½ teaspoon hot sauce
¼ teaspoon salt

1. In a large skillet, sauté onion, garlic, and collard greens in olive oil for 3–5 minutes until onion is soft.

2. Add water or Vegetable Broth, tomatoes, and Cajun seasoning. Bring to a simmer, cover, and allow to cook for 20 minutes, or until greens are soft, stirring occasionally.

3. Remove lid, stir in hot sauce and salt, and cook, uncovered, for another 1–2 minutes to allow excess moisture to evaporate.

🔥 HOW TO PREPARE COLLARDS

Give your collards a good rinse, then tear the leaves off the middle stem. Fold or roll all the leaves together, then run a knife through them to create thin strips, similar to a chiffonade cut used for herbs. The stems can be added to a Vegetable Broth or your compost pile.

Chipotle Corn on the Cob

The corn husks resulting from this spicy recipe can be dried out and reused as a tamale casing.

1. Place the corn in a 4-quart slow cooker and cover with water until it is 1" from the top of the slow cooker.

2. Cook on high heat for 2 hours.

3. While the corn is cooking, combine the vegan margarine, chipotle powder, and salt in a small bowl. When the corn is done cooking, rub a small spoonful of the vegan margarine mixture on each cob and then serve.

Serves 6

6 ears corn, shucked
Water, as needed
3 tablespoons vegan margarine
½ teaspoon chipotle powder
½ teaspoon salt

Cilantro-Lime Corn on the Cob

This pressure cooker Cilantro-Lime Corn on the Cob recipe couldn't be easier—or more delicious! To add a little more kick, increase the amount of cayenne pepper.

Serves 4

4 ears fresh sweet corn, shucked
½ cup water
2 tablespoons vegan margarine, such as Earth Balance
2 tablespoons chopped cilantro
2 teaspoons fresh lime juice
½ teaspoon salt
2 teaspoons cayenne pepper

1. Place the rack in the pressure cooker and place the corn on the rack. Pour in the water.

2. Lock the lid into place and bring to low pressure; maintain pressure for 3 minutes. Remove the pressure cooker from heat, quick-release the pressure, and remove the lid.

3. In a small bowl, combine the margarine, cilantro, lime juice, salt, and cayenne pepper until well blended.

4. When the corn is cool enough to handle, spread ¼ of the mixture on each ear of corn.

Coconut Cauliflower Curry

To save time chopping, substitute a bag of mixed frozen veggies or toss in some leftover cooked potatoes when making this tropical yellow curry recipe.

1. Whisk together the Vegetable Broth and coconut milk in a large saucepan.

2. Add remaining ingredients except the pineapple and cilantro, stirring well to combine. Bring to a slow simmer, cover, and cook for 8–10 minutes, stirring occasionally. Add pineapple and heat for 2 more minutes.

3. Top with fresh cilantro if desired, and serve hot over rice or another whole grain.

Serves 4

¾ cup Vegetable Broth (see Chapter 4)
1 cup coconut milk
1½ cups green peas
1 head cauliflower, chopped
2 carrots, chopped small
2 teaspoons minced fresh ginger
3 cloves garlic, minced
2 teaspoons curry powder
½ teaspoon turmeric
1 teaspoon brown sugar
¼ teaspoon salt
¼ teaspoon nutmeg
1 cup diced pineapple
2 tablespoons chopped fresh cilantro (optional)

Spicy Creamed Spinach

You might not think that spinach would have much taste, but add red pepper flakes and your mouth will be telling a different story!

Serves 6

1 tablespoon vegan margarine
1 clove garlic, minced
1 tablespoon flour
1 cup unsweetened soymilk
½ teaspoon salt
½ teaspoon red pepper flakes
¼ teaspoon dried sage
1 (12-ounce) package frozen spinach, thawed

1. Melt the vegan margarine in a 2-quart slow cooker over high heat. Add the garlic, and cook for 2 minutes before stirring in the flour.

2. Slowly pour in the soymilk and whisk until all lumps are removed.

3. Add all remaining ingredients. Stir, and cook over low heat for 1–2 hours.

♨ VARIATIONS

You can simplify this recipe by going with a simple vegan margarine sauce that is flavored with salt, pepper, and sage, or make this savory dish even richer by adding a sprinkling of vegan cheese such as Daiya Mozzarella Style Shreds.

Spicy Turnip Greens

In this spicy pressure cooker recipe be sure to use fresh or frozen turnip greens for best flavor and optimal nutrition.

1. To prepare the greens, cut away the tough stalks and stems. Wash greens, chop into large pieces, and set aside.

2. Bring the pressure cooker to medium heat. Add the olive oil, onion, garlic, and red pepper flakes. Cook until the onion begins to soften, about 5 minutes. Add the Vegetable Broth, mustard, and chopped greens; stir well.

3. Lock the lid into place and bring to high pressure; maintain for 5 minutes. Remove from heat and release pressure naturally. Add salt and pepper, to taste.

Serves 4

1 pound turnip greens
1 tablespoon olive oil
½ onion, diced
1 clove garlic, minced
1 teaspoon red pepper flakes
2 cups Vegetable Broth (see Chapter 4)
1 teaspoon Dijon mustard
Salt and pepper, to taste

Black and Green Veggie Burritos

Black bean burritos filled with zucchini or yellow summer squash. Just add in the fixings—salsa, avocado slices, some nondairy sour cream . . . the works!

Serves 4

1 onion, chopped
2 zucchinis or yellow squash, cut into thin strips
1 bell pepper, any color, chopped
2 tablespoons olive oil
½ teaspoon oregano
½ teaspoon cumin
1 (15-ounce) can black beans, drained
1 (4-ounce) can green chilies
1 cup cooked rice
4 large flour tortillas, warmed

1. Heat onion, zucchinis or yellow squash, and bell pepper in olive oil until vegetables are soft, about 4–5 minutes.

2. Reduce heat to low and add oregano, cumin, black beans, and green chilies, combining well. Cook, stirring, until well combined and heated through.

3. Place ¼ cup rice in the center of each flour tortilla and top with the bean mixture. Fold the bottom of the tortilla up, then snugly wrap one side, then the other.

4. Serve as is, or bake in a 350°F oven for 15 minutes for a crispy burrito.

🌶 GLUTEN-FREE BEAN BURRITOS

If you're gluten-free or just want an extra protein and nutrition boost, use a cooked grain other than rice in these burritos and shop for a gluten-free flatbread to wrap it up in. Quinoa in particular works well in burritos, as it is lighter than other grains.

Fiery Basil and Eggplant Stir-Fry

Holy basil, called tulsi, is revered in Vishnu temples across India and is frequently used in ayurvedic healing. It lends a fantastically spicy flavor, but regular basil will also do.

1. Sauté the garlic, chili peppers, and tofu in olive oil for 4–6 minutes until tofu is lightly golden.

2. Add eggplant, bell pepper, mushrooms, water, and soy sauce and heat, stirring frequently, for 5–6 minutes, or until eggplant is almost soft.

3. Add lemon juice and basil and cook for another 1–2 minutes, just until basil is wilted.

Serves 3

3 cloves garlic, minced
3 small fresh chili peppers, minced
1 (16-ounce) block firm or extra-firm tofu, pressed and diced
2 tablespoons olive oil
1 eggplant, chopped
1 red bell pepper, chopped
⅓ cup sliced mushrooms
3 tablespoons water
2 tablespoons soy sauce
1 teaspoon lemon juice
⅓ cup fresh Thai basil or holy basil

🔥 TYPES OF BASIL

Sweet Italian basil may be the most common, but other varieties can add a layer of sensually enticing flavor. Lemon basil is identifiable by its lighter green color and fresh, citrusy scent. For this recipe, look for spicy holy basil or Thai basil with a purplish stem and jagged leaf edge for a delightfully scorching flavor.

Eggplant Caponata

Serve this spicy food on small slices of Italian bread as an appetizer, or use as a filling in sandwiches or wraps.

Serves 8

2 (1-pound) eggplants
1 teaspoon olive oil
1 red onion, diced
4 cloves garlic, minced
1 stalk celery, diced
2 tomatoes, diced
2 tablespoons nonpareil capers
2 tablespoons toasted pine nuts
1 teaspoon red pepper flakes
¼ cup red wine vinegar

1. Pierce the eggplants with a fork. Cook on high in a 4- or 6-quart slow cooker for 2 hours.

2. Allow to cool. Peel off the skin. Slice each in half and remove the seeds. Discard the skin and seeds.

3. Place the pulp in a food processor. Pulse until smooth. Set aside.

4. Heat the oil in a nonstick skillet. Sauté the onion, garlic, and celery until the onion is soft, about 5 minutes.

5. Add the eggplant and tomatoes. Sauté 3 minutes.

6. Return to the slow cooker and add the capers, pine nuts, red pepper flakes, and vinegar. Stir. Cook on low 30 minutes. Stir prior to serving.

🔥 CAPERS

Capers are found on a flowering bush and the flower bud is what is commonly called the "caper." They are often pickled and used in a variety of sauces and salads.

Spicy "Baked" Eggplant

Serve this spicy eggplant as a main dish over rice or as a side dish as is.

Place all ingredients in a 1½- to 2-quart slow cooker. Cook on low for 3 hours, or until the eggplant is tender.

 COLD SNAP

Take care not to put a cold ceramic slow cooker insert directly into the slow cooker. The sudden shift in temperature can cause it to crack. If you want to prepare your ingredients the night before use, refrigerate them in reusable containers, not in the insert.

Serves 4

1 pound eggplant, cubed
⅓ cup sliced onion
1 teaspoon red pepper flakes
½ teaspoon crushed rosemary
¼ cup lemon juice

Garlic and Gingered Green Beans

This recipe doesn't use a lot of red pepper flakes, but a little can go a long way when it comes to taste!

Serves 4

1 pound fresh green beans, trimmed and chopped
2 tablespoons olive oil
4 cloves garlic, minced
1 teaspoon fresh minced ginger
1 teaspoon red pepper flakes
Salt and pepper, to taste

1. Boil green beans in water for just 3–4 minutes; do not overcook. Or steam for 4–5 minutes. Drain and rinse under cold water.

2. Heat olive oil in a skillet with garlic, ginger, green beans, and red pepper flakes. Cook, stirring frequently, for 3–4 minutes until garlic is soft.

3. Taste, and season lightly with salt and pepper.

Warm Jicama Slaw

Jicama is a crunchy root vegetable that is typically served cold but also works well in warm dishes because it retains its crunchy texture.

1. Combine the lime juice, water, orange juice, oil, vinegar, and red pepper flakes in a small bowl and stir until well combined.

2. Add the jicama, cabbage, and carrots to a 4-quart slow cooker, add the liquid, and stir. Cover, and cook over low heat for 1 hour.

Serves 6

¼ cup lime juice
¼ cup water
¼ cup orange juice
2 tablespoons vegetable oil
1 teaspoon vinegar
2 teaspoons red pepper flakes
2 cups peeled and shredded jicama
1 cup shredded cabbage
1 cup peeled and shredded carrots

Mango and Bell Pepper Stir-Fry

Add some marinated tofu to make this spicy recipe a main dish, or enjoy just the mango and veggies for a light lunch. Use thawed frozen cubed mango if you can't find fresh.

Serves 4

2 tablespoons lime juice
2 tablespoons orange juice
1 tablespoon hot sauce
3 tablespoons soy sauce
2 cloves garlic, minced
2 tablespoons oil
1 red bell pepper, chopped
1 yellow or orange bell pepper
1 bunch broccoli, chopped
1 mango, cubed
3 scallions, chopped

1. Whisk together the lime juice, orange juice, hot sauce, and soy sauce.

2. Heat garlic in oil for just 1–2 minutes, then add bell peppers and broccoli and cook, stirring frequently, for another 2–3 minutes.

3. Add juice and soy sauce mixture, reduce heat, and cook for another 2–3 minutes until broccoli and bell peppers are almost soft.

4. Reduce heat to low and add mango and scallions, gently stirring to combine. Heat for just another 1–2 minutes until mango is warmed.

Stuffed Bell Peppers

The cuisine of Mexico inspired this version of stuffed bell peppers, but you can prepare the versatile peppers with an Italian twist instead.

1. Combine all of the ingredients except the bell peppers and vegan cheese in a medium bowl and stir until well combined.

2. To prepare the bell peppers, cut the tops off of each and scoop out the pulp and seeds. Stuff each pepper with ¼ of the bread crumb mixture.

3. Arrange the bell peppers so they are standing upright in a 4-quart slow cooker. Sprinkle with the vegan cheese, cover, and cook on low heat for 4–6 hours.

Serves 4

1 cup crumbled soy chorizo
1 cup diced Roma tomatoes
¼ teaspoon garlic powder
1 teaspoon chili powder
½ teaspoon salt
½ cup diced red onion
3 cups plain dry bread crumbs
4 green bell peppers
½ cup shredded vegan Cheddar cheese

Mexican Spice Potatoes

If you like things spicy, really kick it up by adding an extra teaspoon of cayenne to these potatoes!

Serves 4

6 cups cubed red potatoes
1 teaspoon chili powder
½ teaspoon sugar
½ teaspoon paprika
⅛ teaspoon cayenne pepper
⅛ teaspoon garlic powder
¼ teaspoon cumin
½ teaspoon salt
⅛ teaspoon black pepper
½ cup water

Add all ingredients to a 4-quart slow cooker. Cover, and cook on high heat for 4 hours.

Potato Messaround

"Messaround" means a little bit of everything, which is what this slow-cooker recipe has! Try playing with it by adding different cheeses and hot peppers, or swap out the Vegetable Broth and soup, to your taste.

1. Add all of the ingredients to a 4-quart slow cooker except for the chives.

2. Cover, and cook on high heat for 4–5 hours. Garnish with the chives.

Serves 4

8 cups cubed red potatoes
1 red onion, diced
1 poblano pepper, diced
1 red bell pepper, diced
1 jalapeño pepper, minced
3 cups Vegetable Broth (see Chapter 4)
1 (14.5-ounce) can vegan cream of mushroom soup
1 teaspoon salt
¼ teaspoon black pepper
1 cup vegan Cheddar cheese
2 tablespoons chives

Potatoes Paprikash

This spicy Hungarian classic is the perfect side dish to serve with a seitan roast.

Serves 8

1½ teaspoons olive oil
1 medium onion, halved and sliced
1 shallot, minced
4 cloves garlic, minced
½ teaspoon salt
½ teaspoon caraway seeds
¼ teaspoon freshly ground black pepper
1 teaspoon cayenne pepper
3 tablespoons paprika
2 pounds red potatoes, thinly sliced
2 cups Vegetable Broth (see Chapter 4)
2 tablespoons tomato paste
½ cup vegan sour cream

1. In a nonstick pan, heat the oil. Add the onion, shallot, and garlic and sauté for 1–2 minutes, or until they begin to soften. Add the salt, caraway seeds, black pepper, cayenne pepper, and paprika, and stir. Immediately remove from heat.

2. Add the onion mixture, potatoes, Vegetable Broth, and tomato paste to a 4-quart slow cooker. Stir to coat the potatoes evenly.

3. Cover, and cook on high for 2½ hours, or until the potatoes are tender.

4. Turn off the heat and stir in the vegan sour cream.

Potato and Veggie Fritters

These easy potato fritters are similar to an Indian snack called bajji or pakoras. To get the idea, add a few shakes of some Indian spices: curry, turmeric, or garam masala.

1. Boil potatoes until cooked, about 20 minutes. Drain and allow to cool.

2. Mash potatoes together with soymilk, flour, garlic powder, onion powder, chili powder, cumin, cayenne pepper, veggies, salt, and pepper until mixture is thick and potatoes are well mashed, adding a little less soymilk and more flour as needed. Mixture should be dry but sticky.

3. Form into patties and pan-fry in oil over medium heat for 3–4 minutes on each side or until browned and crispy.

Serves 3

3 medium potatoes
Water for boiling
¼ cup soymilk
¼–⅓ cup flour
½ teaspoon garlic powder
½ teaspoon onion powder
½ teaspoon chili powder
½ teaspoon cumin
½ teaspoon cayenne pepper
½ cup frozen peas, corn, and diced carrots mix
Salt and pepper, to taste
Oil for frying

Cilantro Potato and Pea Curry

This spicy dish is a simple curried potato recipe with peas. Turn up the heat by adding in some fresh chilies, or sweeten it for kids by adding some pineapple.

Serves 4

3 cloves garlic
¼ cup water
¼ cup tomato paste
1 teaspoon minced fresh ginger
2 tablespoons curry powder
2 tablespoons cayenne pepper
1 teaspoon sugar (optional)
2 tablespoons soy sauce
½ onion, chopped
1 tablespoon sesame oil
4 medium potatoes, chopped
2 tablespoons olive oil
1½ cups frozen green peas, thawed
1 (14-ounce) can coconut milk
3 tablespoons chopped fresh cilantro

1. Combine garlic, water, tomato paste, ginger, curry powder, sugar if desired, soy sauce, onion, and sesame oil in a blender or food processor and process until smooth.

2. In a large skillet, sauté potatoes in olive oil for 3–4 minutes, then add spice mix and peas and simmer, covered, for 10–12 minutes, stirring occasionally.

3. Add coconut milk and simmer for another 5–6 minutes, stirring well to combine.

4. Remove from heat and add fresh cilantro.

Southwestern Casserole

Serve up this spicy dish taco-style! You can scoop this casserole into warmed corn tortillas for an easy, handheld serving option.

1. In a 4-quart slow cooker, stir all ingredients together except the vegan cheese.

2. Cover, and cook on low for 8–9 hours.

3. Stir in the cheese shortly before serving.

🔥 VEGAN CHEDDAR CHEESE

There are several varieties of vegan Cheddar cheese for sale in grocery stores around the country, but the one that melts, stretches, and tastes the best is Daiya Cheddar Style Shreds.

Serves 6

4 large red potatoes, diced
1 (15-ounce) can black beans, drained
1 large onion, diced
1 jalapeño, seeded and diced
1 tablespoon vegan margarine
1 (15-ounce) can diced tomatoes
4 ounces button mushrooms, sliced
¼ teaspoon salt
¼ teaspoon pepper
¼ cup shredded vegan Cheddar cheese

Polenta and Chili Casserole

Using canned chili and thawed frozen veggies, you can get this spicy, one-pot casserole meal in the oven in just about 10 minutes.

Serves 4

3 cans vegan chili (or about 6 cups homemade)

2 cups diced veggie mixture, any kind

1 cup cornmeal

2½ cups water

2 tablespoons vegan margarine

1 tablespoon chili powder

1. Combine vegan chili and vegetables and spread in the bottom of a lightly greased casserole dish.

2. Preheat oven to 375°F.

3. Over low heat, combine cornmeal and water. Simmer, stirring frequently, for 10 minutes. Stir in vegan margarine.

4. Spread cornmeal mixture over chili and sprinkle the top with chili powder.

5. Bake uncovered for 20–25 minutes.

Lime-Soaked Poblanos

Simple and fresh, this easy recipe can be used as the filling for tacos or burritos, or as a topping on a nopalitos (cactus) salad.

Combine all of the ingredients in a 4-quart slow cooker and stir until well combined. Cover, and cook on low heat for 4 hours.

Serves 4

¼ cup lime juice
¼ cup water
2 cloves garlic, minced
2 tablespoons chopped fresh
   cilantro
½ teaspoon salt
4 poblano peppers, seeded and
   sliced

Spicy Chipotle and Thyme Mashed Sweet Potatoes

To substitute fresh thyme for dried thyme in this spicy pressure-cooker recipe, use ½ tablespoon of the fresh herb.

Serves 4–6

2 cups water
6 cups cubed sweet potatoes
4 tablespoons vegan margarine, such as Earth Balance
3 cloves garlic, minced
½ teaspoon dried chipotle pepper
½ teaspoon dried thyme
Salt and pepper, to taste

1. Pour water into the pressure cooker and add potatoes. Lock the lid into place and bring to high pressure. Once achieved, turn the heat to low and cook for 5 minutes. Remove from heat and release pressure naturally.

2. Drain the potatoes into a colander. Add the margarine to the pressure cooker and sauté the garlic for about 2 minutes. Remove the pressure cooker from the heat. Add the sweet potatoes, chipotle pepper, and thyme. Mash the potatoes using a potato masher or electric mixer. Season with salt and pepper, to taste.

Baked Sweet Potato Fries

Brown sugar adds a sweet touch to these yummy sweet potato fries. If you like your fries with a kick, add some red pepper flakes to the mix.

1. Preheat oven to 400°F.

2. Spread sweet potatoes on a large baking sheet and drizzle with olive oil, tossing gently to coat.

3. In a small bowl, combine remaining ingredients. Sprinkle over potatoes, coating evenly and tossing as needed.

4. Bake in oven for 10 minutes, turning once. Taste, and sprinkle with a bit more sea salt if needed.

Serves 3

2 large sweet potatoes, sliced into fries
2 tablespoons olive oil
¼ teaspoon garlic powder
½ teaspoon paprika
½ teaspoon brown sugar
½ teaspoon chili powder
¼ teaspoon sea salt
½ teaspoon cayenne pepper

Spicy Summer Squash Sauté

Green zucchinis and yellow squash absorb the spicy flavors in this recipe like magic, though little enhancement is needed with their fresh, natural flavor. Toss these veggies with some cooked orzo or linguine to make it a main dish.

Serves 2

1 onion, chopped
2 cloves garlic, minced
2 tablespoons olive oil
2 zucchinis, sliced into coins
2 yellow squash, sliced thin
1 large tomato, diced
2 teaspoons Italian seasoning
1 tablespoon nutritional yeast
2 teaspoons hot sauce

1. Sauté onion and garlic in olive oil for 1–2 minutes, then add zucchinis, yellow squash, and tomato. Heat, stirring frequently, for 4–5 minutes until squash is soft.

2. Season with Italian seasoning and heat for 1 more minute.

3. Stir in nutritional yeast and hot sauce.

CHAPTER 6

Pasta, Rice, Grains, and Beans

PASTA

Easy Pad Thai Noodles

Hot and Spicy Garlic Pasta

Artichoke and Olive Puttanesca

Eggplant and Habanero Puttanesca

Sweet and Spicy Peanut Noodles

Fusilli with Grilled Eggplant, Garlic, and Spicy Tomato Sauce

RICES AND GRAINS

Baked Mexican Rice Casserole

Cuban Black Beans, Sweet Potatoes, and Rice

Curried Rice and Lentils

Indonesian Fried Rice (Nasi Goreng)

Mexican Rice with Corn and Peppers

Spicy Southern Jambalaya

Creole Jambalaya

Spanish Rice

Bell Peppers Stuffed with Couscous

BEANS AND LENTILS

Pumpkin and Lentil Curry

Hot and Spicy Black Bean Burgers

Black Bean Polenta Cakes with Salsa

New Orleans Red Beans and Rice

Indian-Spiced Chickpeas with Spinach (Chana Masala)

Maple Baked Beans

Spicy Falafel Patties

Easy Pad Thai Noodles

Volumes could be written about Thailand's national dish. It's sweet, sour, spicy, and salty all at once, and filled with as much texture and flavor as the streets of Bangkok themselves.

Serves 4

1 pound thin rice noodles
Hot water for soaking
¼ cup tahini
¼ cup ketchup
¼ cup soy sauce
2 tablespoons white, rice, or cider vinegar
3 tablespoons lime juice
2 tablespoons sugar
1 teaspoon red pepper flakes or cayenne pepper
1 (16-ounce) block firm or extra-firm tofu, diced small
3 cloves garlic
¼ cup vegetable or safflower oil
4 scallions, chopped
½ teaspoon salt
Optional toppings: bean sprouts, crushed toasted peanuts, extra scallions, sliced lime

1. Cover the noodles in hot water and set aside to soak until soft, about 5 minutes.

2. Whisk together the tahini, ketchup, soy sauce, vinegar, lime juice, sugar, and red pepper flakes or cayenne.

3. In a large skillet, fry the tofu and garlic in oil until tofu is lightly golden browned. Add noodles, stirring to combine well, and fry for 2–3 minutes.

4. Reduce heat to medium and add tahini and ketchup sauce mixture, stirring well to combine. Allow to cook for 3–4 minutes until well combined and heated through. Add scallions and salt and heat 1 more minute, stirring well.

5. Serve with bean sprouts, crushed toasted peanuts, extra chopped scallions, and 1–2 lime wedges if desired.

🔥 **TRULY THAI**

Pad thai is supposed to be a bit greasy—which is why the noodles are fried in the oil. If you're not worried about fat and have quick-cooking thin rice noodles, you can omit the presoaking in water and just toss the noodles in with the tofu and garlic and add extra oil.

Hot and Spicy Garlic Pasta

It's not fancy, but that's the beauty of this spicy recipe, which is, aptly, for those times when you're too hungry to cook and just want to fill your stomach.

1. Heat the garlic in olive oil for just 1–2 minutes until almost browned.

2. Toss garlic and olive oil with remaining ingredients. Adjust seasonings, to taste.

Serves 6

2 cloves garlic, minced
2 tablespoons olive oil
3 cups pasta, cooked
2 tablespoons nutritional yeast
½ teaspoon parsley
2 tablespoons red pepper flakes
Salt and pepper, to taste

🔥 REALLY HUNGRY? REALLY LAZY?

Garlic powder, nutritional yeast, and salt is a delicious seasoning combination, and will give you a bit of a B_{12} perk-up. Use it over toast, veggies, popcorn, bagels, baked potatoes, and, of course, cooked pasta!

Artichoke and Olive Puttanesca

Use fresh basil and parsley if you have it on hand, but otherwise, dried will taste fine in this delicious, spice-filled dish.

Serves 6

3 cloves garlic, minced
2 tablespoons olive oil
1 (14-ounce) can diced or crushed tomatoes
¼ cup sliced black olives
¼ cup sliced green olives
1 cup chopped artichoke hearts
2 tablespoons capers
1½ teaspoons red pepper flakes
½ teaspoon basil
¾ teaspoon parsley
¼ teaspoon salt
1 (12-ounce) package pasta, cooked

1. Heat garlic in olive oil for 2–3 minutes. Reduce heat and add remaining ingredients except pasta.

2. Cook over low heat uncovered for 10–12 minutes until most of the liquid from tomatoes is absorbed.

3. Toss with cooked pasta.

Eggplant and Habanero Puttanesca

This salty and spicy puttanesca is a thick sauce traditionally served over pasta, but try it over a more wholesome grain, such as quinoa or even brown rice.

1. In a large skillet or saucepan, sauté the garlic, habanero pepper, and eggplant in olive oil for 4–5 minutes until eggplant is almost soft. Add capers, olives, and red pepper flakes, and stir to combine.

2. Reduce heat to low and add remaining ingredients. Cover, and allow to simmer for 10–12 minutes until juice from tomatoes has reduced.

3. Serve over cooked pasta or rice.

Serves 4

3 cloves garlic, minced
1 habanero pepper, chopped
1 eggplant, chopped
2 tablespoons olive oil
2 tablespoons capers, rinsed
⅓ cup sliced kalamata or black olives
½ teaspoon red pepper flakes
1 (14-ounce) can diced tomatoes
1 tablespoon balsamic vinegar
½ teaspoon parsley

Sweet and Spicy Peanut Noodles

Like a siren song, these noodles entice you with their sweet pineapple flavor, then scorch your tongue with fiery chilies. Very sneaky, indeed.

Serves 4

1 (12-ounce) package Asian-style noodles
⅓ cup peanut butter
2 tablespoons soy sauce
⅔ cup pineapple juice
2 cloves garlic, minced
1 teaspoon grated fresh ginger
½ teaspoon salt
1 tablespoon olive oil
1 teaspoon sesame oil
2–3 small chilies, minced
¾ cup diced pineapple

1. Prepare noodles according to package instructions and set aside.

2. In a small saucepan, stir together the peanut butter, soy sauce, pineapple juice, garlic, ginger, and salt over low heat, just until well combined.

3. Place the olive oil and sesame oil in a large skillet and fry chilies and pineapple for 2–3 minutes, stirring frequently, until pineapple is lightly browned. Add noodles and fry for another minute, stirring well.

4. Reduce heat to low and add peanut butter sauce mixture, stirring to combine well. Heat for 1 more minute until well combined.

Fusilli with Grilled Eggplant, Garlic, and Spicy Tomato Sauce

Smoky, fruity flavors of grilled or roasted eggplant marry beautifully with tomatoes and garlic. Fusilli's deep crannies scoop up every drop of this spicy, complex sauce.

1. Heat grill, grill pan, or broiler. Toss the eggplant wedges with 1 tablespoon olive oil; season liberally with salt and pepper. Grill or broil it on the largest cut side for 4 minutes until black marks show. Using tongs or a fork, turn to another side and cook 3 minutes more until it is bubbling with juices. Transfer to a cutting board to cool; cut into 1" pieces.

2. Mix remaining olive oil with garlic and red pepper flakes. Heat a large skillet over medium-high heat. Add the garlic mixture; allow to sizzle just 15 seconds, stirring with a wooden spoon, before adding the parsley. Cook 30 seconds; add the eggplant and tomato sauce. Bring to a simmer, add the cooked pasta, and cook until heated through; remove from heat. Finish by adding margarine and vegan cheese, adjusting for seasoning and tossing well to combine. Serve in bowls, sprinkled with additional chopped parsley. Pass additional vegan cheese on the side if desired.

Serves 4

1 small eggplant (about ½ pound), cut lengthwise into 8 wedges
3 tablespoons olive oil, divided
Kosher salt and freshly ground black pepper
3 cloves garlic, finely chopped (about 1 tablespoon)
1 teaspoon red pepper flakes
½ cup roughly chopped Italian parsley
4 cups tomato sauce
½ box (½ pound) fusilli or other pasta shape, cooked "al dente"
1 tablespoon vegan margarine
¼ cup grated vegan Parmesan cheese

Baked Mexican Rice Casserole

You can get this quick and spicy side dish into the oven in just a few minutes. It doesn't get easier to heat up a weeknight!

Serves 4

1 (15-ounce) can black beans
¾ cup salsa
2 teaspoons chili powder
1 teaspoon cumin
½ cup corn kernels
2 cups rice, cooked
⅓ cup sliced black olives
½ cup grated vegan cheese
(optional)

1. Preheat oven to 350°F.

2. Combine the beans, salsa, chili powder, and cumin in a large pot over low heat, and partially mash beans with a large fork.

3. Remove from heat and stir in corn and rice. Transfer to a casserole dish.

4. Top with sliced olives and vegan cheese if desired and bake for 20 minutes.

🔥 IS YOUR SOY CHEESE VEGAN?

Many nondairy products do actually contain dairy, even if it says "nondairy" right there on the package! Nondairy creamer and soy cheeses are notorious for this. Look for casein or whey on the ingredients list, particularly if you suffer from dairy allergies, and if you're allergic to soy, look for nut- or rice-based vegan cheeses.

Cuban Black Beans, Sweet Potatoes, and Rice

Stir some plain steamed rice right into the pot, or serve it alongside these spicy beans.

1. In a large skillet or pot, sauté garlic and sweet potatoes in olive oil for 2–3 minutes.

2. Reduce heat to medium-low and add beans, Vegetable Broth, chili powder, paprika, and cumin. Bring to a simmer, cover, and allow to cook for 25–30 minutes until sweet potatoes are soft.

3. Stir in lime juice and hot sauce, to taste. Serve hot over rice.

Serves 4

3 cloves garlic, minced

2 large sweet potatoes, chopped small

2 tablespoons olive oil

2 (15-ounce) cans black beans, drained

¾ cup Vegetable Broth (see Chapter 4)

1 tablespoon chili powder

1 teaspoon paprika

1 teaspoon cumin

1 tablespoon lime juice

Hot sauce, to taste

2 cups rice, cooked

Curried Rice and Lentils

With no added fat, this is a very simple one-pot side dish starter recipe. Personalize it with some chopped greens, browned seitan, or a veggie mix.

Serves 4

1½ cups uncooked white or brown rice
1 cup lentils
2 tomatoes, diced
3½ cups water or Vegetable Broth (see Chapter 4)
1 bay leaf (optional)
1 tablespoon curry powder
½ teaspoon cumin
½ teaspoon turmeric
½ teaspoon garlic powder
Salt and pepper, to taste (optional)

1. Combine all ingredients except salt and pepper in a large soup pot or stockpot. Bring to a slow simmer, then cover, and cook for 20 minutes, stirring occasionally, until rice is done and liquid is absorbed.

2. Taste, then add a bit of salt and pepper if needed. If used, remove bay leaf before serving.

🔥 STUFF IT!

Rice makes excellent stuffing for poblano or green bell peppers. Carefully remove the tops of the bell peppers, or, for poblanos, slice down the middle. Fill with cooked curried rice and lentils or Mexican Rice with Corn and Peppers (see recipe in this chapter) and bake at 375°F for 25 minutes or 15 minutes for poblano peppers.

Indonesian Fried Rice (Nasi Goreng)

Like any fried rice recipe, the vegetables you use are really up to you so feel free to be creative.

1. Whisk together the molasses and soy sauce, and set aside.

2. In a large skillet, sauté the tempeh, onion, garlic, and chili in oil for a few minutes until tempeh is lightly browned. Add rice and sesame oil, stirring to combine.

3. Add remaining ingredients, including molasses and soy sauce, and quickly stir to combine.

4. Cook for just a few minutes, stirring constantly, just until heated through.

Serves 6

2 teaspoons molasses
2 tablespoons soy sauce
1 block tempeh, cubed
1 onion, diced
3 cloves garlic, minced
1 small chili, minced
3–4 tablespoons vegetable oil
    or peanut oil
3 cups rice, cooked
1 tablespoon sesame oil
2 tablespoons ketchup
2 tablespoons hot sauce
2 scallions, chopped
1 carrot, sliced thin
1 jalapeño, diced
Dash Chinese five-spice powder

🔥 A WARUNG FAVORITE

In "warungs" (restaurants) across Indonesia, "nasi goreng" is guaranteed to be on the menu, as it's a favorite of visitors and locals alike. Top it off with some extra hot sauce to spice it up and some sliced cucumbers to cool it back down. Browse an Asian grocery store for "kecap manis," a sugary sauce you can use in place of the soy sauce and molasses mixture for a more authentic taste.

Mexican Rice with Corn and Peppers

Although Mexican rice is usually just a filling for burritos or served as a side dish, this spicy recipe loads up the veggies, making it hearty enough for a main dish. Use frozen or canned veggies if you need to save time.

Serves 4

2 cloves garlic, minced
1 cup uncooked rice
2 tablespoons olive oil
3 cups Vegetable Broth (see Chapter 4)
1 cup tomato paste or 4 large tomatoes, puréed
1 green bell pepper, chopped
1 red bell pepper, chopped
Kernels from 1 ear of corn
1 carrot, diced
1 teaspoon chili powder
½ teaspoon cumin
⅓ teaspoon oregano
⅓ teaspoon cayenne pepper
⅓ teaspoon salt

1. Add garlic, rice, and olive oil to a large skillet and heat on medium-high heat, stirring frequently. Toast the rice until just golden brown, about 2–3 minutes.

2. Reduce heat and add Vegetable Broth and remaining ingredients.

3. Bring to a simmer, cover, and allow to cook until liquid is absorbed and rice is cooked, about 20–25 minutes, stirring occasionally.

4. Adjust seasonings, to taste.

 VEGAN BURRITOS

Brown some vegetarian chorizo or mock sausage crumbles and wrap in tortillas, perhaps topped with some shredded vegan cheese, to make vegan burritos. Or, combine with TVP Taco "Meat" (see Chapter 7) to turn this into a "meaty" Mexican main dish.

Spicy Southern Jambalaya

Make this spicy and smoky Southern rice dish a main meal by adding some browned mock sausage or sautéed tofu.

1. In a large skillet or stockpot, heat onion, bell pepper, and celery in olive oil until almost soft, about 3 minutes.

2. Reduce heat and add remaining ingredients except corn or frozen veggies and cayenne or hot sauce. Cover, bring to a low simmer, and cook for 20 minutes until rice is done, stirring occasionally.

3. Add corn or frozen veggies if desired and cayenne or hot sauce and cook just until heated through, about 3 minutes. Adjust seasonings, to taste.

🔥 GOT LEFTOVERS?

Heat up some refried beans and wrap up your leftover jambalaya in tortillas with some salsa and shredded lettuce to make vegan burritos!

Serves 6

1 onion, chopped
1 bell pepper, any color, chopped
1 rib celery, diced
2 tablespoons olive oil
1 (14-ounce) can diced tomatoes, undrained
3 cups water or Vegetable Broth (see Chapter 4)
2 cups rice
1 bay leaf
1 teaspoon paprika
½ teaspoon thyme
½ teaspoon oregano
½ teaspoon garlic powder
1 cup corn or frozen mixed diced veggies (optional)
½ teaspoon cayenne pepper or hot sauce, to taste

Creole Jambalaya

Try Morningstar Farms Meal Starters Chik'n Strips and Tofurky sausage as an alternative to real meat in this hot and spicy pressure cooker recipe.

Serves 8

½ cup vegan margarine, such
   as Earth Balance
1 cup chopped onion
1 medium bell pepper, chopped
2 stalks celery, chopped
3 cloves garlic, minced
3 cups Vegetable Broth (see
   Chapter 4)
1 cup water
1 (8-ounce) can tomato sauce
2 cups white rice
2 bay leaves
2 teaspoons thyme
2 teaspoons cayenne pepper
2 teaspoons Cajun seasoning
Salt, to taste

1. Melt the margarine in the pressure cooker over medium-low heat, then add the onion, bell pepper, celery, and garlic. Cook for about 15 minutes until soft.

2. Add the Vegetable Broth, water, tomato sauce, rice, bay leaves, thyme, cayenne, and Cajun seasoning, then stir.

3. Lock the lid into place; bring to high pressure and maintain for 6 minutes. Remove from heat and allow pressure to release naturally.

4. Season with salt, to taste.

🔥 CREOLE CUISINE

Creole cuisine is similar to, but more refined than, Cajun cooking, and both use the "holy trinity" of onion, bell pepper, and celery as the base of many dishes. The cuisine hails from southern Louisiana, but is influenced by Spanish, French, and African cuisines.

Spanish Rice

Cooking rice in tomatoes, chili powder, and bell pepper is the key to this slow-cooker Spanish rice.

Add all ingredients to a 4-quart slow cooker. Cover, and cook on low heat for 4–5 hours.

Serves 8

2 cups uncooked white rice
2 tablespoons vegan margarine
2 cups water
2 cups Vegetable Broth (see Chapter 4)
1 onion, diced
1 green bell pepper, diced
1 cup diced canned tomatoes
⅛ cup diced pickled jalapeños
1 teaspoon chili powder
½ teaspoon garlic powder
1 teaspoon salt
¼ teaspoon black pepper

Bell Peppers Stuffed with Couscous

Baked stuffed peppers are always a hit with those who appreciate presentation, and this spicy recipe takes very little effort.

Serves 4

4 cups water or Vegetable Broth (see Chapter 4)
3 cups couscous
2 tablespoons olive oil
2 tablespoons lemon or lime juice
1 cup frozen peas or corn, thawed
2 green onions, sliced
½ teaspoon cumin
½ teaspoon chili powder
4 green bell peppers

1. Preheat oven to 350°F.

2. Bring water or Vegetable Broth to a boil and add couscous. Cover, turn off heat, and let sit for 10–15 minutes until couscous is cooked. Fluff with a fork.

3. Combine couscous with olive oil, lemon or lime juice, peas or corn, green onions, cumin, and chili powder.

4. Cut the tops off the bell peppers and remove seeds.

5. Stuff couscous into bell peppers and place the tops back on, using a toothpick to secure if needed.

6. Transfer to a baking dish and bake for 15 minutes.

Pumpkin and Lentil Curry

Red lentils complement the pumpkin and coconut best in this salty-sweet curry, but any kind you have on hand will do. Look for frozen chopped squash to cut the preparation time.

1. Sauté onion and pumpkin or squash in olive oil until onion is soft, about 4 minutes. Add curry powder, cumin, chilies or red pepper flakes, and cloves, and toast for 1 minute, stirring frequently.

2. Reduce heat slightly and add water or Vegetable Broth and lentils. Cover, and cook for about 10–12 minutes, stirring occasionally.

3. Uncover, and add tomatoes, green beans, and coconut milk, stirring well to combine. Heat uncovered for 4–5 more minutes, just until tomatoes and beans are cooked.

4. Serve over rice or whole grains.

Serves 3

1 yellow onion, chopped
2 cups chopped pumpkin or
    butternut squash
2 tablespoons olive oil
1 tablespoon curry powder
1 teaspoon cumin
2 small red chilies, minced, or ½
    teaspoon red pepper flakes
2 whole cloves
3 cups water or Vegetable Broth
    (see Chapter 4)
1 cup lentils
2 tomatoes, chopped
8–10 fresh green beans,
    trimmed and chopped
¾ cup coconut milk

Hot and Spicy Black Bean Burgers

Veggie burgers are notorious for falling apart. If you're sick of crumbly burgers, try this simple method for making these hot and spicy black bean patties. It's 100-percent guaranteed to stick together.

Yields 6 patties

1 (15-ounce) can black beans, drained
3 tablespoons minced onions
1 teaspoon salt
1½ teaspoons garlic powder
2 teaspoons parsley
1½ teaspoons chili powder
⅔ cup flour
Oil for pan-frying
1 tablespoon hot sauce, for garnish

1. Process the black beans in a blender or food processor until halfway mashed, or mash with a fork.

2. Add minced onions, salt, garlic powder, parsley, and chili powder and mash to combine.

3. Add flour, a bit at a time, again mashing together to combine. You may need a little bit more or less than ⅔ cup. Beans should stick together completely.

4. Form into patties and pan-fry in a bit of oil for 2–3 minutes on each side. Patties will appear to be done on the outside while still a bit mushy on the inside, so fry them a few minutes longer than you think they need. Top with hot sauce.

🔥 VEGGIE BURGER TIPS

Although this recipe is foolproof, if you have trouble with your veggie burgers crumbling, try adding egg replacer to bind the ingredients, then chill the mixture before forming into patties. Veggie burger patties can be grilled, baked, or pan-fried, but they do tend to dry out a bit in the oven. Not a problem; just smother with extra ketchup!

Black Bean Polenta Cakes with Salsa

All the flavors of the Southwest combine in this colorful confetti polenta loaf. Pan-fry individual slices if you like, or just enjoy it as it is.

1. Place black beans in a bowl and mash with a fork until halfway mashed. Set aside.

2. Bring the water to a boil, then slowly add cornmeal, stirring to combine.

3. Reduce heat to low and cook for 10 minutes, stirring frequently and scraping the bottom of the pot to prevent sticking and burning.

4. Add bell pepper, cumin, chili powder, garlic powder, oregano, salt, and pepper and stir well to combine. Continue to heat, stirring frequently for 8–10 more minutes.

5. Add vegan margarine and stir well to combine, then add black beans, combining well.

6. Gently press into a lightly greased loaf pan, smoothing the top with the back of a spoon. Chill until firm, at least 1 hour. Reheat, slice, and serve topped with prepared salsa.

Serves 4

1 (15-ounce) can black beans, drained
6 cups water
2 cups cornmeal
½ red or yellow bell pepper, diced small
¾ teaspoon cumin
1 teaspoon chili powder
1 teaspoon garlic powder
¾ teaspoon oregano
½ teaspoon salt
½ teaspoon black pepper
2 tablespoons vegan margarine
Salsa

New Orleans Red Beans and Rice

This spicy, slow-cooker dish is a New Orleans staple that is traditionally served on Mondays.

Serves 8

¼ cup vegan margarine
1 cup diced onion
1 cup diced green bell pepper
1 cup diced celery
5 cloves garlic, minced
2 (15-ounce) cans red kidney beans, drained
1½ cups water
4 teaspoons salt
2 teaspoons liquid smoke
1 teaspoon vegan Worcestershire sauce
2 teaspoons hot sauce
1 teaspoon dried thyme
2 teaspoons cayenne pepper
4 bay leaves
8 cups cooked long-grain white rice

1. Add the vegan margarine to a 4-quart slow cooker and sauté the onion, green bell pepper, celery, and garlic for 3–5 minutes over high heat.

2. Add the red kidney beans, water, salt, liquid smoke, Worcestershire sauce, hot sauce, dried thyme, cayenne pepper, and bay leaves. Cover, and cook on low heat for about 6 hours.

3. Remove the bay leaves and serve over the cooked white rice.

Indian-Spiced Chickpeas with Spinach (Chana Masala)

This spicy recipe is enjoyable as is for a side dish or piled on top of rice or another grain for a main meal.

1. In a large skillet, sauté onion, garlic, and jalapeño in margarine until almost soft, about 2 minutes.

2. Reduce heat to medium-low and add coriander, cumin, and cayenne pepper. Toast the spices, stirring, for 1 minute.

3. Add the chickpeas with liquid in can, tomatoes or tomato paste, curry powder, turmeric, and salt and bring to a slow simmer. Allow to cook until most of the liquid has been absorbed, about 10–12 minutes, stirring occasionally, then add lemon juice.

4. Add spinach and stir to combine. Cook just until spinach begins to wilt, about 1 minute. Serve immediately.

Serves 3

1 onion, chopped
2 cloves garlic, minced
1 jalapeño, minced
2 tablespoons vegan margarine
¾ teaspoon coriander
1 teaspoon cumin
½ teaspoon cayenne pepper
1 (15-ounce) can chickpeas, undrained
3 tomatoes, puréed, or ⅔ cup tomato paste
½ teaspoon curry powder
¼ teaspoon turmeric
¼ teaspoon salt
1 tablespoon lemon juice
1 bunch fresh spinach

Maple Baked Beans

Tailor these saucy, spicy Boston-style baked beans to your liking by adding extra molasses or some TVP crumbles for a meaty texture.

Serves 6

3 cups navy or pinto beans
9 cups water
1 onion, chopped
⅔ cup maple syrup
¼ cup barbecue sauce
2 tablespoons molasses
1 tablespoon Dijon mustard
1 tablespoon chili powder
1 tablespoon cayenne pepper
1 teaspoon paprika
1½ teaspoons salt
¾ teaspoon pepper

1. Cover beans in water and allow to soak at least 8 hours or overnight.

2. Preheat oven to 350°F.

3. Drain beans. In a large Dutch oven or sturdy pot, combine beans and remaining ingredients. Bring to a rolling boil on the stove.

4. Cover, and bake beans for 1½ hours, stirring once or twice. Uncover, and cook 1 more hour.

5. Alternatively, beans can be simmered over low heat for 1½–2 hours on the stovetop.

Spicy Falafel Patties

Health food stores sell a vegan instant falafel mix, but it's not very much work at all to make your own from scratch.

1. Preheat oven to 375°F.

2. Place chickpeas in a large bowl and mash with a fork until coarsely mashed or pulse in a food processor until chopped.

3. Combine chickpeas with onion, flour, cumin, garlic, salt, and egg replacer, mashing together to combine. Add parsley and cilantro if desired.

4. Shape mixture into 2" balls or 1"-thick patties and bake in oven for 15 minutes or until crisp. Falafel can also be fried in oil for about 5–6 minutes on each side.

5. Stuff falafel into a pita bread with some sliced tomatoes and lettuce and top it off with Roasted Red Pepper Hummus.

Serves 4

1 (15-ounce) can chickpeas, well drained
½ onion, minced
1 tablespoon flour
1 teaspoon cumin
¾ teaspoon garlic powder
¾ teaspoon salt
Egg replacer for 1 egg
¼ cup chopped fresh parsley
2 tablespoons chopped fresh cilantro (optional)
Pita bread
¼ tomato, sliced
Lettuce, for garnish
2 tablespoons Roasted Red Pepper Hummus (see Chapter 3)

CHAPTER 7

Tofu, Seitan, TVP, and Tempeh

TOFU

Barbecue Tofu

Blackened Tofu

Cajun-Spiced Cornmeal-Breaded Tofu

Chili and Curry Baked Tofu

General Tso's Tofu

Indian Tofu Palak

Mexican Spice–Crusted Tofu

Mexico City Protein Bowl

Orange-Glazed "Chicken" Tofu

Saag Tofu Aloo

Panang Tofu

Saucy Kung Pao Tofu

Simmered Coconut Curried Tofu

Spicy Chili Basil Tofu

Sticky Teriyaki Tofu Cubes

Thai Tofu Coconut Curry

Tofu Barbecue Sauce "Steaks"

SEITAN AND TVP

Massaman Curried Seitan

Apples and Onions Seitan

Seitan Barbecue "Meat"

Seitan Buffalo Wings

Sinless Chili Cheese Fries

"Sloppy Jolindas" with TVP

Cashew Seitan

Spicy Seitan Taco "Meat"

TVP Taco "Meat"

Pineapple TVP Baked Beans

Confetti "Rice" with TVP

TEMPEH

Baked Mexican Tempeh Cakes

Cajun Tempeh Po'boys

"Short Rib" Tempeh

Spicy Tempeh Fajitas

Sriracha and Soy Tempeh

Tempeh Jambalaya

Tempeh Tamale Pie

Curried "Chicken" Salad

Barbecue Tofu

Serve this barbecue tofu with a side of baked beans and coleslaw, or use it as the filling for a delicious sandwich served on a hoagie.

Serves 4

4 cups ketchup
½ cup apple cider vinegar
1 cup water
½ cup vegan Worcestershire
   sauce
½ cup light brown sugar, firmly
   packed
¼ cup molasses
¼ cup prepared mustard
2 tablespoons barbecue
   seasoning
1 teaspoon freshly ground black
   pepper
1 tablespoon liquid smoke
1 tablespoon hot sauce
1 (16-ounce) package extra-firm
   tofu, pressed and quartered

1. In a large bowl, combine all the ingredients except the tofu. Pour the mixture into the slow cooker and add the tofu, making sure that it is fully covered with sauce.

2. Set the slow cooker to high and cook for 1–2 hours, flipping the tofu at the halfway point.

Blackened Tofu

Preparing this spicy Blackened Tofu on the grill is a delicious alternative to using a slow cooker on a warm summer day.

1. Place the tofu, soy sauce, vinegar, and garlic in a small bowl and allow to marinate for 10 minutes.

2. To make the blackened seasoning mixture, combine the paprika, black pepper, salt, garlic powder, cayenne, oregano, and thyme in a small bowl. Remove the tofu from the soy marinade and dip each side into the blackened seasoning.

3. Add the oil and blackened tofu to a 2-quart slow cooker. Cover, and cook on low heat for 4 hours.

Serves 4

2 (16-ounce) packages extra-firm tofu, pressed and quartered
⅓ cup soy sauce
1 tablespoon apple cider vinegar
1 tablespoon minced garlic
1 tablespoon paprika
2 teaspoons black pepper
1½ teaspoons salt
1 teaspoon garlic powder
1 teaspoon cayenne pepper
½ teaspoon dried oregano
½ teaspoon dried thyme
2 tablespoons vegetable oil

🔥 TYPES OF TOFU

Most major grocery stores carry two different types of tofu— regular or silkened. Regular tofu is what you should always use unless the recipe specifically calls for silkened, which is most common in desserts or recipes where the tofu needs a creamy consistency.

Cajun-Spiced Cornmeal-Breaded Tofu

Reminiscent of oven-fried breaded catfish, this is a spicy, southern-inspired breaded tofu that can be baked or fried.

Serves 3

⅔ cup soymilk
2 tablespoons lime juice
¼ cup flour
⅓ cup cornmeal
1 tablespoon Cajun seasoning
1 teaspoon onion powder
½ teaspoon cayenne pepper, or
    to taste
½ teaspoon salt
½ teaspoon black pepper
1 (16-ounce) block firm or
    extra-firm tofu, well pressed

1. Preheat oven to 375°F and lightly grease a baking pan.

2. Combine soymilk and lime juice in a wide shallow bowl. In a separate bowl, combine flour, cornmeal, Cajun seasoning, onion powder, cayenne, salt, and pepper.

3. Slice tofu into triangles or rectangular strips and dip in soymilk and lime juice mixture. Next, coat well with cornmeal and flour mixture.

4. Transfer to baking pan and bake for 8–10 minutes on each side. Serve with hot sauce or barbecue sauce.

5. Alternatively, you can pan-fry in a bit of oil for 2–3 minutes on each side.

Chili and Curry Baked Tofu

If you like tofu and you like Indian- or Thai-style curries, you'll love this spicy baked tofu, which tastes like a slowly simmered curry in each bite. Use the extra marinade to dress a bowl of plain steamed rice.

1. Whisk together coconut milk, garlic powder, cumin, curry, turmeric, chilies, and maple syrup in a shallow bowl. Add tofu and marinate for at least 1 hour, flipping once or twice to coat well.

2. Preheat oven to 425°F.

3. Transfer tofu to a casserole dish in a single layer, reserving marinade.

4. Bake for 8–10 minutes. Turn tofu over and spoon 1–2 tablespoons of marinade over the tofu. Bake 10–12 more minutes.

Serves 3

⅓ cup coconut milk
½ teaspoon garlic powder
1 teaspoon cumin
1 teaspoon curry powder
½ teaspoon turmeric
2–3 small chilies, minced
2 tablespoons maple syrup
1 (16-ounce) block firm or extra-firm tofu, sliced into thin strips

General Tso's Tofu

The combination of sweet and spicy is what makes this dish a hit at Chinese restaurants across the country.

Serves 2

1 (16-ounce) package extra-firm tofu, pressed and cubed
1 cup water
2 tablespoons cornstarch
2 cloves garlic, minced
1 teaspoon minced ginger
⅛ cup sugar
2 tablespoons soy sauce
⅛ cup white wine vinegar
⅛ cup sherry
2 teaspoons cayenne pepper
2 tablespoons vegetable oil
2 cups chopped broccoli

Add all ingredients to a 4-quart slow cooker. Cover, and cook on medium heat for 4 hours.

Indian Tofu Palak

Palak paneer is a popular Indian dish of creamed spinach and soft cheese. This version uses tofu for a similarly spicy dish.

1. Heat tofu and garlic in olive oil over low heat and add nutritional yeast and onion powder, stirring to coat tofu. Heat for 2–3 minutes until tofu is lightly browned.

2. Add spinach, water, curry, cumin, and salt, stirring well to combine. Once spinach starts to wilt, add soy yogurt and heat just until spinach is fully wilted and soft.

Serves 4

1 (16-ounce) block firm or
   extra-firm tofu, cut into small
   cubes
3 cloves garlic, minced
2 tablespoons olive oil
2 tablespoons nutritional yeast
½ teaspoon onion powder
4 bunches fresh spinach
3 tablespoons water
1 tablespoon curry powder
2 teaspoons cumin
½ teaspoon salt
½ cup plain soy yogurt

Mexican Spice–Crusted Tofu

These little bites are packed with spices, so no dipping sauce is needed, but feel free to dip in hot sauce if you want to spice this dish up even more.

Serves 3

3 tablespoons soy sauce
3 tablespoons hot sauce
1 teaspoon sugar
1 (16-ounce) block firm or extra-firm tofu, sliced into strips
1 teaspoon garlic powder
1 teaspoon onion powder
1 tablespoon chili powder
¾ teaspoon cumin
¾ teaspoon oregano
2 tablespoons flour

1. Whisk together the soy sauce, hot sauce, and sugar in a shallow pan and add tofu. Marinate tofu for at least 1 hour.

2. In a separate dish, combine the garlic powder, onion powder, chili powder, cumin, oregano, and flour to form a spice rub. Carefully dip each piece of tofu in the spices on each side, then transfer to a lightly greased baking sheet.

3. Bake at 350°F for 7–9 minutes, turning once.

🔥 PRESSING TOFU

Tofu doesn't taste like much on its own, but soaks up spices and marinades wonderfully. It's like a sponge: the drier it is, the more flavor it absorbs. Wrap firm tofu in a couple layers of paper towels and place a can of beans or another light weight on top. After 10 minutes, flip the tofu over and let it sit weighted down for another 10 minutes. "Pressing" firm and extra-firm tofu will substantially enhance just about every recipe.

Mexico City Protein Bowl

This spicy dish is a quick meal for one in a bowl, reminiscent of Mexico City street food stalls, but healthier!

1. Heat tofu and scallion in olive oil for 2–3 minutes, then add peas, corn, and chili powder. Cook another 1–2 minutes, stirring frequently.

2. Reduce heat to medium-low and add black beans. Heat for 4–5 minutes until well combined and heated through.

3. Place 2 corn tortillas in the bottom of a bowl and spoon beans and tofu over the top. Season with hot sauce, to taste.

Serves 1

½ (16-ounce) block firm tofu, diced small
1 scallion, chopped
1 tablespoon olive oil
½ cup peas
½ cup corn kernels
½ teaspoon chili powder
1 can black beans, drained
2 corn tortillas
Hot sauce, to taste

Orange-Glazed "Chicken" Tofu

If you're missing Chinese restaurant–style orange-glazed chicken, try this easy tofu version. Double the sauce and add some veggies for a full meal over rice.

Serves 3

⅔ cup orange juice
2 tablespoons soy sauce
2 tablespoons rice vinegar
1 tablespoon maple syrup
½ teaspoon red pepper flakes
2 tablespoons olive oil
1 (16-ounce) block firm or
    extra-firm tofu, well pressed
3 cloves garlic, minced
1½ teaspoons cornstarch
2 tablespoons water

1. Whisk together the orange juice, soy sauce, vinegar, maple syrup, and red pepper flakes, and set aside.

2. In a large skillet, heat the oil and add tofu and garlic. Lightly fry just a few minutes over medium heat.

3. Reduce heat to medium-low and add in orange-juice mixture. Bring to a very low simmer and allow to cook for 7–8 minutes over low heat.

4. Whisk together the cornstarch and water in a small bowl until cornstarch is dissolved. Add to tofu mixture, stirring well to combine.

5. Bring to a simmer and heat for 3–4 minutes until sauce thickens. Serve over rice or another whole grain if desired.

Saag Tofu Aloo

Saag Tofu Aloo is a fresh-tasting, protein-rich Indian dish that is only slightly spicy. "Saag" means "spinach" and "aloo" means "potato."

1. Cut the tofu into ½" cubes. Set aside.

2. Heat the oil in a nonstick skillet. Add the cumin seeds and sauté for 1 minute.

3. Add the garlic and jalapeños. Sauté until fragrant, about 1 minute.

4. Add the tofu and potatoes. Sauté for 3 minutes.

5. Add the ginger, garam masala, frozen spinach, and cilantro. Sauté 1 minute.

6. Pour the mixture into a 4-quart slow cooker and cook for 4 hours on low.

Serves 4

1 (16-ounce) package extra-firm tofu
1 tablespoon canola oil
1 teaspoon cumin seeds
2 cloves garlic, minced
2 jalapeños, minced
¾ pound red potatoes, diced
½ teaspoon ground ginger
¾ teaspoon garam masala
1 pound frozen cut leaf spinach
¼ cup fresh cilantro

🔥 SERVING SUGGESTIONS

There are many different ways to enjoy Indian dishes such as this one. Try it over a bed of rice, scoop it up with naan (flatbread), or roll it up in chapati (another type of flatbread).

Panang Tofu

Panang is typically a red curry that is often milder than other curries, but this recipe spices it up by adding extra peppers.

Serves 2

1 (16-ounce) package extra-firm tofu, pressed and cubed
1 (13-ounce) can coconut milk
1 tablespoon panang curry paste
2 tablespoons soy sauce
1 tablespoon lime juice
2 tablespoons sugar
2 tablespoons olive oil
¼ onion, sliced
½ carrot, sliced diagonally
½ red bell pepper, chopped
½ habanero pepper, chopped
½ cup chopped fresh basil

1. Add all ingredients except the basil to a 4-quart slow cooker.

2. Cover, and cook on low heat for 4–6 hours.

3. Add the basil before serving.

Saucy Kung Pao Tofu

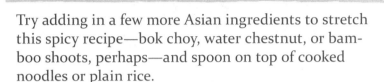

Try adding in a few more Asian ingredients to stretch this spicy recipe—bok choy, water chestnut, or bamboo shoots, perhaps—and spoon on top of cooked noodles or plain rice.

1. Whisk together the soy sauce, rice vinegar or sherry, and sesame oil in a shallow pan or ziplock bag. Add tofu and marinate for at least 1 hour—the longer, the better. Drain tofu, reserving marinade.

2. Sauté bell peppers, mushrooms, garlic, chili peppers, and red pepper flakes in oil for 2–3 minutes, then add tofu and heat for another 1–2 minutes until veggies are almost soft.

3. Reduce heat to medium-low and add marinade, ground ginger, water or Vegetable Broth, sugar, and cornstarch, whisking in the cornstarch to avoid lumps.

4. Heat a few more minutes, stirring constantly, until sauce has almost thickened.

5. Add green onions and peanuts and heat for 1 more minute.

Serves 6

3 tablespoons soy sauce
2 tablespoons rice vinegar or cooking sherry
1 tablespoon sesame oil
2 (16-ounce) blocks firm or extra-firm tofu
1 red bell pepper, chopped
1 green bell pepper, chopped
⅔ cup sliced mushrooms
3 cloves garlic
3 small red or green chili peppers, diced small
1 teaspoon red pepper flakes
2 tablespoons oil
1 teaspoon ground ginger
½ cup water or Vegetable Broth (see Chapter 4)
½ teaspoon sugar
1½ teaspoons cornstarch
2 green onions, chopped
½ cup peanuts

Simmered Coconut Curried Tofu

Serve this spicy dish on top of rice or pasta. It's delicious either way!

Serves 3

1 (16-ounce) block firm or extra-firm tofu, cubed
1 tablespoon olive oil
2 teaspoons sesame oil
3 tablespoons peanut butter
2 tablespoons soy sauce
2 tablespoons water
1 teaspoon curry powder
¼ cup coconut flakes
2 tablespoons minced fresh cilantro

1. Sauté tofu in olive oil for just a few minutes until lightly golden brown.

2. Reduce heat to medium-low and add sesame oil, peanut butter, soy sauce, water, and curry powder, stirring well to combine. Heat, gently stirring, for 4–5 minutes.

3. Add coconut flakes and cilantro and heat just until well combined, about 1 more minute.

Spicy Chili Basil Tofu

This saucy stir-fry is a favorite in Thailand when made with chicken and fish sauce, but many restaurants offer a vegan version with soy sauce and tofu instead. Serve with rice or rice noodles to sop up all the sauce.

1. In a large skillet, sauté garlic, chilies, and shallots in oil until fragrant and browned, about 3–4 minutes.

2. Add tofu and heat for another 2–3 minutes until tofu is just lightly golden brown.

3. Reduce heat to medium-low and add soy sauce, mushroom sauce, and sugar, whisking to combine and dissolve sugar. Heat 2–3 more minutes, stirring frequently, then add basil and heat, stirring 1 more minute, just until basil is wilted.

Serves 3

4 cloves garlic, minced
5 small red or green chilies, diced
3 shallots, diced
2 tablespoons oil
1 (16-ounce) block firm tofu, diced
¼ cup soy sauce
1 tablespoon vegan oyster mushroom sauce
1 teaspoon sugar
1 bunch Thai or holy basil leaves

🔥 MAKE IT LAST

If tofu and chilies aren't enough for you, add in some onions, mushrooms, or green bell peppers to fill it out. Or, for a bit of variety, try it with half basil and half fresh mint leaves.

Sticky Teriyaki Tofu Cubes

Cut tofu into wide slabs or triangular cutlets for a main dish or smaller cubes to add to a salad, or just for an appetizer or snack.

Serves 3

⅓ cup soy sauce

3 tablespoons barbecue sauce

2 teaspoons hot sauce

¼ cup maple syrup

¾ teaspoon garlic powder

1 (16-ounce) block firm or extra-firm tofu, cut into thin chunks

1. Preheat oven to 375°F.

2. In a casserole or baking dish, whisk together the soy sauce, barbecue sauce, hot sauce, maple syrup, and garlic powder.

3. Add tofu and cover with sauce.

4. Bake for 35–40 minutes, tossing once.

Thai Tofu Coconut Curry

Try this deliciously hot, easy curry tossed with rice noodles or over brown rice.

1. Slice the tofu into ½"-thick triangles.

2. Place the tofu into a 4-quart slow cooker. Top with coconut, water, garlic, ginger, galangal, onion, sweet potato, broccoli, snow peas, tamari, vegan fish sauce, and chili-garlic sauce.

3. Stir to distribute all ingredients evenly. Cook on low for 5 hours.

4. Stir in the cilantro and coconut milk. Cook on low for an additional 20 minutes. Stir prior to serving.

Serves 6

1 (16-ounce) package extra-firm tofu
¼ cup unsweetened shredded coconut
¼ cup water
4 cloves garlic, minced
1 tablespoon minced fresh ginger
1 tablespoon minced galangal root
½ cup chopped onion
1 cup peeled and diced sweet potato
1 cup broccoli florets
1 cup snow peas
3 tablespoons tamari
1 tablespoon vegan fish sauce
1 tablespoon chili-garlic sauce
½ cup minced fresh cilantro
½ cup light coconut milk

Tofu Barbecue Sauce "Steaks"

These spicy tofu "steaks" have a hearty texture and a meaty flavor. It's delicious as is, or add it to a sandwich. If you've never cooked tofu before, this is a supereasy, foolproof recipe to start with.

Serves 3

⅓ cup barbecue sauce

¼ cup water

2 teaspoons balsamic vinegar

2 tablespoons soy sauce

1–2 tablespoons hot sauce, or to taste

2 teaspoons sugar

2 (16-ounce) blocks firm or extra-firm tofu, well pressed

½ onion, chopped

2 tablespoons olive oil

1. In a small bowl, whisk together the barbecue sauce, water, vinegar, soy sauce, hot sauce, and sugar until well combined. Set aside.

2. Slice pressed tofu into ¼"-thick strips.

3. Sauté onion in oil, and carefully add tofu. Fry tofu on both sides until lightly golden brown, about 2 minutes on each side.

4. Reduce heat and add barbecue sauce mixture, stirring to coat tofu well. Cook over medium-low heat until sauce absorbs and thickens, about 5–6 minutes.

🔥 TOFU VERSUS SEITAN

This recipe, like many pan-fried or stir-fried tofu recipes, will also work well with seitan, though seitan needs a bit longer to cook all the way through—otherwise it ends up tough and chewy.

Massaman Curried Seitan

With Indian influences and popular among Muslim communities in southern Thailand, Massaman curry is a truly global dish. This version is simplified but still has a distinct kick. Diced tomatoes, baby corn, or green peas would go well in this recipe if you want to add veggies.

1. In a large skillet or stockpot, heat five-spice powder, ginger, turmeric, and cayenne in oil for just 1 minute, stirring constantly, until fragrant.

2. Reduce heat to medium-low and add coconut milk and Vegetable Broth, stirring to combine. Add potatoes, seitan, and cloves; cover, and cook for 15–20 minutes, stirring occasionally.

3. Uncover, add peanut butter, cinnamon, salt, sugar, and peanuts or cashews if desired, and heat for 1 more minute. Serve over rice.

4. If you prefer a thicker curry, dissolve 1 tablespoon cornstarch in 3 tablespoons water and add to curry, simmering for 2–3 minutes until thick.

Serves 4

1 tablespoon Chinese five-spice powder
½ teaspoon grated fresh ginger
½ teaspoon turmeric
¼ teaspoon cayenne pepper, or to taste
1 tablespoon oil
1½ cups coconut milk
1 cup Vegetable Broth (see Chapter 4)
2 potatoes, chopped
1½ cups chopped seitan
2 whole cloves
1 tablespoon peanut butter
¼ teaspoon cinnamon
1 teaspoon salt
2 teaspoons brown sugar
⅓ cup peanuts or cashews (optional)
1 tablespoon cornstarch + 3 tablespoons water (optional)

Apples and Onions Seitan

Try Sonya apples in this dish; they are crisp and sweet.

Serves 4

4 crisp sweet apples, cut into wedges
2 large onions, sliced
1 cup water
4 equal-size seitan cutlets (about 1 pound)
2 teaspoons cayenne pepper
½ teaspoon ground cinnamon
¼ teaspoon allspice
¼ teaspoon ground fennel

1. Place half of the apple wedges and half of the sliced onions in the bottom of a 4-quart slow cooker, then add water. Top with a single layer of seitan.

2. Sprinkle with spices and top with the remaining apples and onions.

3. Cover, and cook on low for 8 hours.

 IN SEASON

Apples are in peak season only once a year, so grab your basket and head to the orchard during the fall. However, you can find good apples during other seasons too. Just check your local supermarket.

Seitan Barbecue "Meat"

Sooner or later, all vegans discover the magically delicious combination of seitan and barbecue sauce in some variation of this classic favorite.

1. Heat seitan, onion, and garlic in oil, stirring frequently, until onion is just soft and seitan is lightly browned.

2. Reduce heat to medium-low and stir in Carolina Barbecue Sauce and water. Allow to simmer, stirring to coat seitan, until most of the liquid has been absorbed, about 10 minutes.

Serves 6

1 package prepared seitan, chopped into thin strips (about 2 cups)
1 large onion, chopped
3 cloves garlic, minced
2 tablespoons oil
1 cup Carolina Barbecue Sauce (see Chapter 2)
2 tablespoons water

🔥 SEITAN SANDWICHES

Piled on top of sourdough along with some vegan mayonnaise, lettuce, and tomato, this recipe makes a perfect sandwich. Melt some vegan cheese for a simple Philly "cheesesteak"-style sandwich, or pile on the vegan Thousand Island dressing and sauerkraut for a seitan Reuben.

Seitan Buffalo Wings

To tame these spicy wings, dip in a cooling dairy-free ranch dressing or serve with chilled cucumber slices.

Serves 4

⅓ cup vegan margarine
⅓ cup Louisiana Hot Sauce
1 cup flour
1 teaspoon garlic powder
1 teaspoon onion powder
¼ teaspoon cayenne pepper
½ cup soymilk
Oil for frying
1 (16-ounce) package seitan or mock chicken, chopped

1. Over low heat, combine the margarine and Louisiana Hot Sauce just until margarine is melted. Set aside.

2. In a small bowl, combine the flour, garlic powder, onion powder, and cayenne pepper. Place soymilk in a separate bowl and heat oil.

3. Dip each piece of seitan in the soymilk, then dredge in flour mixture. Carefully place in hot oil and deep-fry until lightly golden brown on all sides, about 4–5 minutes.

4. Coat fried seitan with margarine and hot sauce mixture.

🔥 BAKED, NOT FRIED

This is, admittedly, not the healthiest of vegan recipes, but you can cut some of the fat out by skipping the breading and deep-frying. Instead, lightly brown the seitan in a bit of oil, then coat with the sauce. Alternatively, bake the seitan with the sauce for 25 minutes at 325°F.

Sinless Chili Cheese Fries

Chili cheese fries *sin carne* (without meat) are almost healthy enough to eat as an entrée. Almost. But go ahead and eat them for dinner—you deserve it, and no one will ever know.

1. Prepare french fries according to package instructions.

2. Sauté onion in oil until soft. Reduce heat and add beans, TVP, tomato paste, chili powder, cumin, and cayenne pepper. Cover, and simmer for 8–10 minutes.

3. In a separate pot, melt the vegan margarine and flour together until thick and pasty, then stir in soymilk, mustard, garlic, and salt. Add vegan cheese and heat just until melted and mixture has thickened.

4. Smother french fries with TVP chili, and top with cheese sauce.

Serves 4

1 (20-ounce) bag frozen french fries
½ onion, chopped
1 tablespoon oil
1 (15-ounce) can kidney beans
1½ cups TVP, rehydrated in water
1⅓ cups tomato paste
2 tablespoons chili powder
½ teaspoon cumin
½ teaspoon cayenne pepper, or to taste
2 tablespoons vegan margarine
2 tablespoons flour
1½ cups soymilk
2 tablespoons prepared mustard
½ teaspoon garlic powder
½ teaspoon salt
½ cup grated vegan cheese

"Sloppy Jolindas" with TVP

"Sloppy Jolindas" with TVP are reminiscent of those goopy sloppy joes served up in primary-school cafeterias, with all of the nostalgic comfort and none of the gristle or mystery meat. The TVP is only partially rehydrated—the better to absorb all the flavors.

Serves 8

1¾ cups TVP

1 cup hot water or Vegetable Broth (see Chapter 4)

1 onion, chopped

1 green bell pepper, chopped small

2 tablespoons oil

1 (16-ounce) can tomato sauce

¼ cup Carolina Barbecue Sauce (see Chapter 2)

2 tablespoons chili powder

1 tablespoon ground mustard

1 tablespoon soy sauce

2 tablespoons molasses

2 tablespoons apple cider vinegar

1 teaspoon hot sauce, or to taste

1 teaspoon garlic powder

½ teaspoon salt

1. Combine the TVP and water or Vegetable Broth and allow to sit at least 5 minutes.

2. In a large soup pot or stockpot, sauté onion and bell pepper in oil until soft.

3. Reduce heat to medium-low and add TVP and remaining ingredients. Simmer, covered, for at least 15 minutes, stirring occasionally.

4. For thicker and less sloppy "Sloppy Jolindas," simmer a bit longer, uncovered, to reduce the liquid.

Cashew Seitan

Hoisin is a soy-based, sweet and spicy sauce that is often used as a glaze for meats in Chinese dishes.

1. Combine the rice wine, hoisin sauce, soy sauce, water, and sugar in a 4-quart slow cooker, stir well, and then add all remaining ingredients except the cashews.

2. Cover, and cook on low for 6 hours. Garnish with cashew pieces before serving.

Serves 6

¼ cup rice wine
½ cup hoisin sauce
¼ cup soy sauce
½ cup water
1 tablespoon sugar
1 (16-ounce) package seitan,
   cut into bite-size pieces
2 tablespoons olive oil
1 red bell pepper, chopped
1 green bell pepper, chopped
4 cloves garlic, minced
½ cup cashew pieces

Spicy Seitan Taco "Meat"

Finely dice the seitan, or pulse it in the food processor until diced small, for maximum surface area and spice in this recipe, and pile up the taco fixings!

Serves 6

½ onion, diced
½ green or red bell pepper, chopped small
1 large tomato, chopped
1 package prepared seitan, chopped small (about 2½ cups)
2 tablespoons oil
1 tablespoon soy sauce
1 teaspoon hot sauce, or to taste
2 teaspoons chili powder
½ teaspoon cumin

1. In a large skillet, sauté onion, bell pepper, tomato, and seitan in oil, stirring frequently, until seitan is browned and tomatoes and pepper are soft.

2. Reduce heat and add soy sauce, hot sauce, chili powder, and cumin, coating well. Heat for 1 more minute.

TVP Taco "Meat"

Whip up this spicy and economical taco filling in just a few minutes using prepared salsa, and have diners fill their own tacos according to their taste. Nondairy sour cream, fresh tomatoes, shredded lettuce, and extra hot sauce are a must, and find some room on your table for sliced avocados or vegan cheese if you can.

1. Combine TVP with hot water and allow to sit for 5–10 minutes to reconstitute. Drain.

2. In a large skillet, heat onion and bell peppers in olive oil. Add TVP, chili powder, and cumin. Cook, stirring frequently, for 4–5 minutes or until peppers and onion are soft.

3. Add salsa and hot sauce, stirring to combine. Remove from heat.

4. Wrap TVP mixture in flour tortillas or spoon into taco shells and serve with taco fillings.

Serves 6

2 cups TVP flakes
2 cups hot water
1 yellow onion, diced
½ red or yellow bell pepper, diced
½ green bell pepper, diced
2 tablespoons olive oil
2 teaspoons chili powder
1 teaspoon cumin
½ cup salsa
½ teaspoon hot sauce, or to taste
6 flour tortillas or taco shells

🔥 TVP: CHEAP, CHEWY, AND MEATY

TVP is inexpensive and has such a meaty texture that many budget-conscious nonvegan cooks use it to stretch their dollar, adding it to homemade burgers and meatloaves. For the best deal, buy it in bulk. TVP is usually found in small crumbles, but some specialty shops also sell it in strips or chunks.

Pineapple TVP Baked Beans

Add a kick to these saucy homemade vegan baked beans by upping the amount of cayenne pepper if you'd like.

Serves 4

2 (15-ounce) cans pinto or navy beans, partially drained
1 onion, diced
⅔ cup barbecue sauce
2 tablespoons prepared mustard
2 tablespoons brown sugar
1 cup TVP
1 cup hot water
1 (8-ounce) can diced pineapple, drained
¾ teaspoon salt
½ teaspoon pepper
½ teaspoon cayenne pepper

1. In a large stockpot, combine beans and about half the liquid, onion, barbecue sauce, mustard, and brown sugar and bring to a slow simmer. Cover, and allow to cook for at least 10 minutes, stirring occasionally.

2. Combine TVP and hot water and allow to sit for 6–8 minutes to rehydrate TVP.

3. Add TVP, pineapple, salt, pepper, and cayenne pepper to beans; cover, and slowly simmer another 10–12 minutes.

Confetti "Rice" with TVP

If your family likes Mexican rice, try this whole-grain version with barley and TVP.

1. In a large skillet, heat the onion and garlic in olive oil for 1–2 minutes, then add barley. Toast for 1 minute, stirring constantly.

2. Add canned tomatoes including liquid, Vegetable Broth, chili powder, and cumin. Cook until barley is almost soft, about 15 minutes.

3. While barley is cooking, combine TVP with hot water or Vegetable Broth and soy sauce and allow to sit for 8–10 minutes until TVP is rehydrated. Drain any excess liquid.

4. When barley is almost done cooking, add rehydrated TVP, veggies, parsley, and salt. Heat for another 5 minutes, or until done.

🔥 TURN IT INTO TACOS

Use this "meaty" Mexican "rice" as a base for burritos or crunchy tacos, along with some shredded lettuce, vegan cheese, and nondairy sour cream, or, serve alongside some cooked beans for a healthy Mexican meal.

Serves 6

1 onion, chopped
2 cloves garlic, minced
2 tablespoons olive oil
1 cup barley
1 (15-ounce) can diced tomatoes
2 cups Vegetable Broth (see Chapter 4)
1 teaspoon chili powder
½ teaspoon cumin
¾ cup TVP
1 cup hot water or Vegetable Broth (see Chapter 4)
1 tablespoon soy sauce
1 cup frozen veggie mix (peas, corn, and carrots)
1 teaspoon parsley
½ teaspoon salt

Baked Mexican Tempeh Cakes

Like tofu, tempeh can be baked in a flavorful sauce, but it does need to be simmered first, just to soften it up a bit.

Serves 4

2 (8-ounce) packages tempeh
1 cup water or Vegetable Broth (see Chapter 4)
⅓ cup tomato paste
3 cloves garlic, minced
2 tablespoons soy sauce
2 tablespoons apple cider vinegar
3 tablespoons water
1½ teaspoons chili powder
½ teaspoon oregano
¼ teaspoon cayenne pepper, or to taste
Tomato salsa or hot sauce

1. If your tempeh is thicker than ¾", slice it in half through the middle to create 2 thinner halves. Then slice each block of tempeh into 4 fillets. Simmer in water or Vegetable Broth for 10 minutes, and drain well.

2. Whisk together the tomato paste, garlic, soy sauce, vinegar, water, chili powder, oregano, and cayenne. Add tempeh, and allow to marinate for at least 1 hour or overnight.

3. Preheat oven to 375°.

4. Transfer tempeh to a lightly greased baking sheet or casserole dish and baste with a bit of the marinade.

5. Bake for 15–17 minutes. Turn tempeh pieces over and baste with a bit more marinade. Bake another 15–17 minutes. Serve topped with tomato salsa or hot sauce.

Cajun Tempeh Po'boys

This hot and spicy recipe makes two very large sandwiches, so bring your appetite or you can save some for later.

1. Add all ingredients except the bread, lettuce, and tomatoes to a 4-quart slow cooker, cover, and cook on high heat for 2 hours.

2. Assemble the sandwiches on the bread by layering the tempeh, lettuce, and tomatoes.

🔥 ALL "DRESSED" UP

Traditional New Orleans po'boys are served either plain or dressed. Dressed means it's topped with lettuce, tomatoes, pickles, and mayo, but you can substitute Vegenaise to keep the sandwich vegan.

Serves 2

1 (13-ounce) package tempeh, cut into small, bite-size squares

½ cup olive oil

5 cloves garlic, minced

1 onion, chopped

2 teaspoons oregano

2 teaspoons thyme

2 teaspoons cayenne pepper

2 tablespoons paprika

1 teaspoon salt

¼ teaspoon black pepper

1 loaf French bread, sliced horizontally

2 cups shredded lettuce

2 tomatoes, sliced

"Short Rib" Tempeh

No pigs necessary for this mouthwatering "rib" recipe!

Serves 4

1 (13-ounce) package tempeh, cut into strips
1 (28-ounce) can tomato sauce
½ cup water
⅛ cup vegan Worcestershire sauce
2 tablespoons brown sugar
2 tablespoons dried parsley
1 teaspoon Tabasco sauce
¼ teaspoon black pepper
Juice of 1 lemon
1 tablespoon soy sauce

Add all ingredients to a 4-quart slow cooker. Cover, and cook on low heat for 6 hours.

Spicy Tempeh Fajitas

Add a dollop of soy sour cream and salsa to finish off each of your fiery fajitas.

1. Add the tempeh, garlic, ginger, soy sauce, water, olive oil, chili powder, chipotle powder, black pepper, onion, green bell pepper, jalapeño, and mushrooms to a 4-quart slow cooker. Cover, and cook on low heat for 6 hours.

2. Serve the fajitas on the tortillas and garnish with tomato, cilantro, and lime.

Serves 4

1 (13-ounce) package tempeh, cut into bite-size pieces
2 cloves garlic, minced
1 teaspoon minced fresh ginger
¼ cup soy sauce
1 cup water
1 tablespoon olive oil
½ teaspoon chili powder
¼ teaspoon chipotle powder
¼ teaspoon black pepper
½ onion, sliced
½ green bell pepper, sliced
1 jalapeño, minced
½ cup sliced mushrooms
8–12 corn tortillas
1 tomato, diced
¼ cup chopped cilantro
1 lime, cut into wedges

Sriracha and Soy Tempeh

Sriracha is sometimes affectionately referred to as "rooster sauce" because of the drawing on the bottle of the most familiar brand, but don't let the cute name fool you; this sauce packs a spicy punch.

Serves 4

1 (13-ounce) package tempeh, cut into bite-size squares
4 cloves garlic, minced
1 teaspoon minced ginger
1 tablespoon olive oil
½ cup soy sauce
¼ cup water
2 tablespoons brown sugar
1 teaspoon sriracha sauce

Add all ingredients to a 4-quart slow cooker, cover, and cook on high heat for 2 hours.

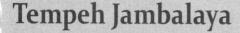

Tempeh Jambalaya

Unlike the famous New Orleans dish gumbo, this spicy jambalaya isn't meant to be brothy; instead you cook the rice dish until all of the liquid is absorbed.

Add all ingredients to a 4-quart slow cooker, cover, and cook on low heat for 6 hours or until all of the liquid is absorbed.

🔥 BAY LEAVES

Bay leaves are often used to flavor soups, stews, and other liquids during cooking. They are typically dried and used whole, but you can also crumble them into a dish and you won't need to remove before serving.

Serves 6

1 (13-ounce) package tempeh, cut into bite-size squares
1 onion, chopped
2 stalks celery, chopped
1 bell pepper, chopped
4 cloves garlic, minced
2 cups uncooked white rice
2 teaspoons Better Than Bouillon No Chicken Base
5 cups water
1 (15-ounce) can tomato sauce
2 bay leaves
⅛ cup Cajun seasoning
¼ teaspoon dried thyme
2 teaspoons hot sauce
1 teaspoon salt
¼ teaspoon black pepper

Tempeh Tamale Pie

In a slight variation from the baked classic, this hot and spicy version of tamale pie features plump, moist cornmeal dumplings.

Serves 4

2 tablespoons olive oil
1 large onion, minced
1 pound tempeh, crumbled
1 jalapeño, minced
2 cloves garlic, minced
1 (15-ounce) can diced tomatoes
1 (10-ounce) can diced tomatoes with green chilies
1 (15-ounce) can dark red kidney beans, drained and rinsed
4 chipotle peppers in adobo, minced
½ teaspoon Mexican chili powder
⅔ cup unsweetened soymilk
2 tablespoons canola oil
2 teaspoons baking powder
½ cup cornmeal
½ teaspoon salt

1. In a large sauté pan over medium heat, add the olive oil. Sauté the onion, tempeh, jalapeño, and garlic for 5 minutes.

2. Pour the tempeh mixture into a 4-quart slow cooker. Add the tomatoes, tomatoes with green chilies, beans, chipotles, and chili powder. Cover, and cook on low for 8 hours.

3. In a medium bowl, mix the soymilk, oil, baking powder, cornmeal, and salt. Drop in ¼-cup mounds in a single layer on top of the tempeh.

4. Cover, and cook on high for 20 minutes without lifting the lid. The dumplings will look fluffy and light when fully cooked.

🔥 CANNED VERSUS FRESH TOMATOES

While fresh tomatoes are delicious, canned tomatoes are a better choice in some recipes because they have already been cooked. Skins and seeds have been removed from canned tomatoes, which is also a bonus when seeds and skin might detract from the dish. There is also reason to believe that canned tomatoes are better sources of cancer-preventing lycopene simply because they are cooked, and that one can of crushed tomatoes or sauce is the equivalent of dozens of fresh tomatoes.

Curried "Chicken" Salad

Turn this spicy "chicken" salad into a sandwich, or slice up some tomatoes and serve on a bed of lettuce.

1. Cover tempeh with water and simmer for 10 minutes until tempeh is soft. Drain and allow to cool completely.

2. Whisk together mayonnaise, lemon juice, garlic powder, mustard, and relish.

3. Combine tempeh, mayonnaise mixture, peas, celery, curry powder, cayenne pepper, and black pepper, and gently toss to combine.

4. Chill for at least 1 hour before serving to allow flavors to combine.

Serves 3

1 (8-ounce) package tempeh, diced small
Water for boiling
3 tablespoons vegan mayonnaise
2 teaspoons lemon juice
½ teaspoon garlic powder
1 teaspoon Dijon mustard
2 tablespoons sweet pickle relish
½ cup green peas
2 stalks celery, diced small
½ teaspoon curry powder
Dash cayenne pepper
Dash black pepper

CHAPTER 8

Hot and Sweet
Desserts and Drinks

DESSERTS

Spiced Chocolate Cake

Spiced Peaches

Spicy Fruit Salad

Mango Chili Sorbet

Bourbon and Chili Brownies

DRINKS

Mexican Hot Chocolate

Bloody Mary Mix

Bloody Maria

Micheladas

Cucumber Margaritas

Hot-Blooded

Prairie Fire Shooter

Spiced Chocolate Cake

Serve this spicy, pressure-cooker chocolate cake with icing, powdered sugar, or vegan ice cream on top.

Serves 10–12

1½ cups all-purpose flour
4 tablespoons cocoa powder
1 teaspoon cinnamon
1 teaspoon cayenne pepper
1 teaspoon sugar
¼ teaspoon salt
1 teaspoon baking powder
2 bananas
4 tablespoons vegan margarine,
    such as Earth Balance
1 cup soymilk
2 cups hot water

1. In a medium bowl, mix the flour, cocoa powder, cinnamon, cayenne, sugar, salt, and baking powder. In a large bowl, mash the bananas. Add the dry ingredients to the bananas. Slowly stir in the melted margarine and the soymilk. Pour the cake mixture into an 8" round pan.

2. Add the steaming rack to the pressure cooker and pour in the hot water. Place the cake in the pressure cooker and lock the lid into place. Bring to high pressure, then reduce to low and cook for 30 minutes.

3. Remove the pressure cooker from the heat, quick-release the steam, and carefully remove the cake.

Spiced Peaches

Spicy and simple to make, these pressure cooker Spiced Peaches will bring a smile to any face.

1. Add all of the ingredients to the pressure cooker. Stir to mix. Lock the lid into place and bring to low pressure; maintain pressure for 3 minutes. Remove the pressure cooker from the heat, quick-release the pressure, and remove the lid. Remove and discard the cinnamon stick, cloves, and peppercorns.

2. Return to medium heat. Simmer and stir for 5 minutes to thicken the syrup. Serve warm or chilled. To store, allow to cool and then refrigerate for up to a week.

Serves 6

2 (15-ounce) cans sliced
   peaches in syrup
¼ cup water
1 tablespoon white wine vinegar
⅛ teaspoon ground allspice
1 cinnamon stick
4 whole cloves
½ teaspoon ground ginger
Pinch cayenne pepper
1 tablespoon minced candied
   ginger
3 whole black peppercorns

 MAKE SPICED PEACH BUTTER

To make spiced peach butter, after Step 2 process the peaches and liquid in a blender or food processor until smooth, and return to the pressure cooker. Simmer and stir over low heat for 30 minutes or until thickened enough to coat the back of a spoon.

Spicy Fruit Salad

Tropical fruit sprinkled with chili powder is a popular street snack in Mexico. Consider this a basic guide, and use any amount and combination of fruits that you like. It's impossible to screw this up.

Yields as many servings as you like

Pineapple, peeled, cored, and cut into cubes

Mango, peeled, cored, and cut into cubes

Watermelon, skin removed, cut into cubes

Papaya, peeled, cored, and cut into cubes

Jicama, peeled and cut into cubes

Fresh lime juice, to taste

Chili powder, to taste

Salt, to taste

1. Place all the fruit in a large, shallow bowl.

2. Squeeze lime juice all over the fruit. Sprinkle generously with chili powder, then sprinkle with salt.

3. Stir the fruit gently to mix ingredients without bruising fruit.

4. Taste and adjust seasoning to your liking.

Mango Chili Sorbet

Based on the Mexican fruit with chili snack, this vegan ice frozen treat is perfect on a hot day. For ultrasmooth ice, purée the mixture 2 or 3 times. Or just enjoy it chunky.

1. Put all ingredients in a blender and process until smooth. You may need to add just a little bit of water.

2. Pour mixture into large bowl. Cover, and put in freezer for 2 hours.

3. Take the mixture out of the freezer and purée in blender again.

4. Freeze mixture again until solid. Serve with an extra sprinkling of chili powder.

Yields 4 servings

8 large mangoes, peeled, pitted, and cut into small cubes
2 cups sugar
¾ cup fresh lime juice
½ teaspoon ancho chili powder

🔥 MANGOES

Mangoes are a tropical fruit that have been cultivated since as far back as 2000 B.C. in India. Today, they are cultivated throughout Southeast Asia, Mexico, South America, and the Caribbean. Because they continue to ripen even after they are picked, mangoes are a popular export crop and have no trouble making long journeys to their final destinations.

Bourbon and Chili Brownies

This recipe yields dense, chewy brownies with spicy hints of chili and bourbon.

Yields 1 dozen big brownies

4 ounces vegan chocolate, roughly chopped
1 stick vegan margarine, softened and cut into little cubes
1 cup sugar
Egg replacer for 2 eggs
½ teaspoon vanilla extract
¼ cup bourbon
½ cup + 1 tablespoon all-purpose flour
⅛ teaspoon salt
¼ teaspoon cinnamon
½ teaspoon ancho chili powder

1. Preheat oven to 350°F. Grease an 8" square baking pan.

2. Combine chocolate and margarine in a small, microwavable bowl. Microwave 20 seconds at a time until melted; stir until smooth. (You can also melt the chocolate and margarine in a small saucepan on the stove.)

3. Transfer chocolate mixture to a large bowl. Add sugar and stir to combine.

4. Add egg replacer and stir until smooth.

5. Add vanilla extract and bourbon, then stir.

6. Add flour, salt, cinnamon, and chili powder. Stir gently until smooth.

7. Pour mixture into baking pan and bake 20–25 minutes until just set in the middle and a toothpick stuck in comes out clean.

8. Let brownies cool before cutting.

Mexican Hot Chocolate

Few things are more comforting on a winter night than a cup of hot cocoa, except this hot cocoa with a little extra spice.

1. Over medium heat, combine all the ingredients in a large saucepan. Whisk constantly until mixture is hot, but not boiling, about 6–8 minutes.

2. Pour into mugs.

Serves 4

4 cups soymilk
½ cup water
8 ounces vegan chocolate, finely chopped
2 tablespoons sugar
1 teaspoon vanilla extract
½ teaspoon chili powder
¼ teaspoon ground cinnamon
Pinch kosher salt

Bloody Mary Mix

Instead of having to make the same drink over and over again, make a batch of this spicy Bloody Mary Mix before having people over for brunch.

Yields enough for 8 Bloody Marys

2 (46-ounce) cans tomato juice
Juice of 2 fresh lemons
2 tablespoons vegan Worcestershire sauce
1 tablespoon horseradish
¼ teaspoon cayenne pepper
½ teaspoon celery salt
½ teaspoon ground black pepper
Tabasco or other hot sauce, to taste

Mix all ingredients and refrigerate. You can add many types of ingredients to this basic Bloody Mary Mix: raw horseradish, lime juice, wasabi, chili powder, bitters, or anything else you like. Go wild. Combine 2 cups Bloody Mary Mix with 1–2 shots of vodka to make a Bloody Mary.

Bloody Maria

The Bloody Mary goes south of the border with tequila and lime instead of vodka and a celery stalk.

1. Run a lime wedge around the rim of a tall glass, then dip the rim in celery salt.

2. Fill the glass with ice and squeeze the same lime wedge into it.

3. Shake the celery salt, vegan Worcestershire sauce, pepper, and Tabasco sauce into the glass.

4. Add the tequila and tomato juice and stir well with a long iced tea or bar spoon. Garnish with a lime wedge.

Serves 1

2 lime wedges
¼ teaspoon celery salt
¼ teaspoon vegan Worcestershire sauce
⅛ teaspoon pepper
Dash Tabasco sauce
1 ounce tequila
5 ounces tomato juice

Micheladas

You can vary the ingredients in this classic Mexican drink to your taste. Try it with different kinds of beer too; dark ale will make a more robust Michelada than a light beer.

Serves 2

1 (16-ounce) bottle beer
2 tablespoons lime juice
¼ teaspoon Tabasco sauce
2 teaspoons vegan Worcester-
    shire sauce
1 tablespoon soy sauce
½ teaspoon salt
2 cups crushed ice

In a cocktail shaker, combine all ingredients except ice and shake to blend well. Strain over ice.

 IN THE LIQUOR STORE

In some liquor stores or grocery stores, you may be able to find a michelada mix to add to cold beer. But the real fun lies in experimenting and adjusting the spices to your liking.

Cucumber Margaritas

Cucumbers offer a mild and cooling contrast in these pretty, light green drinks.

1. Peel cucumbers, cut in half, and remove seeds with a spoon. Cut into chunks and place in blender or food processor with remaining ingredients. Cover, and blend or process until mixture is smooth and thick.

2. Serve immediately.

Serves 6

2 cucumbers
⅓ cup lime juice
2 tablespoons superfine sugar
½ cup tequila
½ teaspoon salt
¼ teaspoon cayenne pepper
1 cup crushed ice

Hot-Blooded

There is a common misconception that lighting a shot on fire concentrates the liquor and makes the drink stronger. In reality, lighting the liquor on fire makes the drink less strong. The fire burns away some of the alcohol and weakens the drink.

Yields 1 shot

1½ ounces tequila
Several dashes Tabasco
⅛ ounce 151 rum

Pour the tequila into a shot glass and add several dashes of Tabasco. Gently layer the 151 rum on top, then light. Allow the flame to die out, then drink.

Prairie Fire Shooter

One taste and you'll understand why they call it fire. You can chase the shooter with a beer to calm the fire.

Pour tequila into a shot glass and add the Tabasco.

Yields 1 shot

1½ ounces tequila
3 dashes Tabasco

🔥 TEQUILA

Tequila is made from the blue agave, a cactus-like plant that grows in the area near the city of Tequila. True tequila must have a blue agave content of 51 percent, otherwise it is called mescal. Fine tequilas are 100 percent blue agave.

Metric Conversion Chart

VOLUME CONVERSIONS	
U.S. Volume Measure	**Metric Equivalent**
⅛ teaspoon	0.5 milliliter
¼ teaspoon	1 milliliter
½ teaspoon	2 milliliters
1 teaspoon	5 milliliters
½ tablespoon	7 milliliters
1 tablespoon (3 teaspoons)	15 milliliters
2 tablespoons (1 fluid ounce)	30 milliliters
¼ cup (4 tablespoons)	60 milliliters
⅓ cup	90 milliliters
½ cup (4 fluid ounces)	125 milliliters
⅔ cup	160 milliliters
¾ cup (6 fluid ounces)	180 milliliters
1 cup (16 tablespoons)	250 milliliters
1 pint (2 cups)	500 milliliters
1 quart (4 cups)	1 liter (about)
WEIGHT CONVERSIONS	
U.S. Weight Measure	**Metric Equivalent**
½ ounce	15 grams
1 ounce	30 grams
2 ounces	60 grams
3 ounces	85 grams
¼ pound (4 ounces)	115 grams
½ pound (8 ounces)	225 grams
¾ pound (12 ounces)	340 grams
1 pound (16 ounces)	454 grams

OVEN TEMPERATURE CONVERSIONS

Degrees Fahrenheit	Degrees Celsius
200 degrees F	95 degrees C
250 degrees F	120 degrees C
275 degrees F	135 degrees C
300 degrees F	150 degrees C
325 degrees F	160 degrees C
350 degrees F	180 degrees C
375 degrees F	190 degrees C
400 degrees F	205 degrees C
425 degrees F	220 degrees C
450 degrees F	230 degrees C

BAKING PAN SIZES

U.S.	Metric
8 × 1½ inch round baking pan	20 × 4 cm cake tin
9 × 1½ inch round baking pan	23 × 3.5 cm cake tin
11 × 7 × 1½ inch baking pan	28 × 18 × 4 cm baking tin
13 × 9 × 2 inch baking pan	30 × 20 × 5 cm baking tin
2 quart rectangular baking dish	30 × 20 × 3 cm baking tin
15 × 10 × 2 inch baking pan	30 × 25 × 2 cm baking tin (Swiss roll tin)
9 inch pie plate	22 × 4 or 23 × 4 cm pie plate
7 or 8 inch springform pan	18 or 20 cm springform or loose bottom cake tin
9 × 5 × 3 inch loaf pan	23 × 13 × 7 cm or 2 lb narrow loaf or pâté tin
1½ quart casserole	1.5 liter casserole
2 quart casserole	2 liter casserole

INDEX